Education and Social Change in Liberia

New Perspectives for the 21st Century

By

Tarnue Carver Johnson

authorHOUSE™

1663 LIBERTY DRIVE, SUITE 200
BLOOMINGTON, INDIANA 47403
(800) 839-8640
WWW.AUTHORHOUSE.COM

First published by AuthorHouse 10/04/04

ISBN: 1-4184-9816-5 (sc)

Printed in the United States of America
Bloomington, Indiana

This book is printed on acid-free paper.

Acknowledgements

This book is an eternal tribute to my late mother, Loupu, who gave me the gift of life for which I am infinitely and eternally grateful. My heart and best wishes also go out to the voiceless and all those who have fallen during a prolonged period of pain and suffering in my beloved Liberia. It is primarily because of them and because of my desire to help create a better tomorrow that I have undertaken to do this project.

Table of Contents

Introduction

This book could not have come at an important time in the political and social history of Liberia. After fourteen years of dwelling in the doldrums, the country today is engaged in a total overhaul through the assiduous efforts of the international community and well-meaning citizens, provided that overhaul takes on specific forms. There seems to be light at the end of the tunnel after a prolonged period of economic and political decline. From past historical experiences one knows that the success of this process depends on the patterns of institutional development adopted. I have had a unique opportunity and vantage perspective in the past four years to air my views through various news organs, both community based and international, as well as peer-reviewed professional journals.

But in this book I now have an added opportunity to weave together the various themes that have constituted my focus of analysis. In other words, I now have the opportunity to present my views in a more coherent and deliberative fashion. These views, which have been undergoing maturation for several years now, have attempted to provide an alternative interpretive perspective in terms of the nature and scope of institutional impediments to social change in Liberian society. My most immediate concerns have been about how to establish the institutional mechanisms for power free dialogue in Liberian civil and political life. Thus, the views and predispositions I have elaborated in this book are also intended to establish a more humane platform for conflict resolution in the political and social spheres. Conflicts are an inseparable part of these spheres, because they are the places where human transactions and associational life take form and character.

I have become more and more convinced through experience and insight that our attempts to fashion viable institutional alternatives for civil dialogue and social change must be situated in the very nature of human rationality and discourse. In this view, I would profess that I have built upon the historical and epistemological foundations laid down by earlier social theorists. Consequently, the basic rationale of the book follows from the assumption that the necessary conditions for free full participation in rational discourse do not exist in Liberia, given the institutional and psychosocial constraints that have existed in the country. It is further suggested, as evidenced throughout the chapters and sections of this book, that these institutional and psychosocial factors are the resultant of the evolution of authority relations in the Liberian society since the 19th century, when the various micro collectivities in the sub-region began to be organized under the rubric of a somewhat homogenous republic and social system.

More specifically, the views expressed in this book broadly fall within the area of adult education research and theory suggested by Taylor and others. Taylor (1998) has suggested the need to foster strategies of transformative learning and social action in varied contexts, taking into consideration socio-cultural and historical forces. Other authors have also variously contributed to this theme, including the earlier generation of critical theorists, Paulo Friere, Jack Mezirow, Stephen Brookfield, Donald Schon, Chris Agyris, etc. My basic analytic approaches and problematic assumptions in this work are anchored in an interdisciplinary perspective. Thus, I have adopted sociological, learning, cognitive and developmental perspectives to gauge the behavior of adults in institutional and bureaucratic systems, because it is adults who principally organize and run these systems. The character of these institutions ultimately reflects the personalities and attitudes of their authors, who happen to be adult members of society. Thus, the failure of these systems is as much reflective of a moral and political failure of adults in society.

Because adult participants are affected by the mores and ethics of these systems in as much as they shape them, a prior assumption critical to an organizing disposition is that institutional and bureaucratic systems are essentially learning systems that can utilize the potential embedded in the structure of human rationality and communication such as critical reflection, epistemic cognition, dialectical thinking and embedded logic (see Brookfield, 1993). Accordingly, the various essays that comprised this book have sought to investigate the impact of the interplay of authority relations and institutional processes on the ideal conditions of discourse, in a society long besieged by cultural, psychosocial, and institutional constraints.

In this particular connection, one of the most compelling objectives of this compilation has been to break a new ground for a paradigmatic approach in the interpretation of institutional, psycho-cultural, and social processes in the Liberian society. This interpretive paradigm must be seen and thus anchored within the sociological and epistemological context of Habermas' communicative rationality and discourse democracy. I can see how this new interpretive perspective, at least within the context of Liberian civil discourses, would ultimately be informed by emerging social and historical circumstances of a nation in continuous flux.

The book starts with chapter one which provides a brief historical survey of Liberia, an overview of the Liberian educational system followed by a comprehensive survey of the underlying theoretical perspectives within which this entire work can be conceptually located. Chapter two provides perspectives on education and emancipatory action in Liberia. The chapter traces the emergence of paternalism in Liberia and the linkage between it and the lack of opportunities for free expression and public discourse in the society. In this chapter I argued that what lies at the heart of social oppression are specific psychosocial and hegemonic assumptions which must be eliminated in order to occasion societal advancement. Chapter three looks at issues surrounding national reconstruction and institutional development in the country. Chapter four is reflective of a cluster of essays that highlight the dynamics of the relationship between education and the building of a viable civic culture and society. Chapter four and five together present a group of essays on current events that focus on how we can develop a road map to the future through participatory discourse and the promotion of critical consciousness in schools and organizational systems throughout the society.

The book concludes in chapter six by making several recommendations for policy action to construct the basis for the development of lifelong learning within the context of a tradition of discourse democracy and social action. This concluding chapter stresses the need for concrete policy action to promote linkages between various levels of education in the country. It also examines the need for deliberate efforts in order to promote peace education to develop capacities for national reconciliation and political sustainability.

I have argued in significant sections of the book that postsecondary institutions should be given financial and material incentives to develop and implement curricular frameworks that incorporate the value of experiential learning, and the cultural knowledge of those participating in educational programs at all levels, including professional training. I am of the view that this would be critical to a campaign of cultural and political renaissance. To develop the theoretical perspectives of transformation as a governing paradigm, new lines of research have been proposed to advance transformation theory in order to increase our conceptual and empirical understanding of the implications of institutional failures for ideal discourse and emancipatory action in non-western societies. I have also underscored the importance that the central government should create an enabling environment through public action to support non-governmental and voluntary associations, to launch study circles in urban and rural areas to enhance associational life, economic productivity, and social action.

The book makes a number of other critical observations regarding the educational system in the country. The educational system in Liberia has failed consistently since its formation in the 19th century to facilitate organized schooling. Similarly, the adult education sector remains undeveloped and largely irresponsive to new historical imperatives and the nascent opportunities to harness lifelong and independent learning, which have emerged in the postwar realties of a struggling nation. Thus, widespread academic underachievement prevails in the face of persistent lack of proper support and misguided efforts to strengthen the process of educational development. Around the 1970s, shifts in World Bank theoretical postures and policy priorities with regards to development assistance for education, compounded preexisting problems of disorganization and systemic malfunctioning. Educational researchers, arguing from a system perspective, have aptly described this lack of cohesion in the education system in Liberia as loose coupling (Weick, 1982).

In the 1980s, a World Bank Group assessment team for the Ministry of Education reported that the Liberian educational system was fractionalized and lacked in coordination between its various constituent elements. Teaching was said to be an autonomous activity often divorce from instructional materials, curriculum planning, and administration (World Bank, 1982). This report glaringly encapsulates the nature and character of an educational system, which must adapt at all levels especially at the tertiary and post-secondary-levels, to accommodate a new progressive tradition of collective social action and educating for perspective transformation and social change. It is this tradition of personal and social transformation that would be critical to the process of transition to a more stable state, in a society that has hitherto failed to meet the great challenges of peaceful coexistence and sustained development in our contemporary epoch.

Part I: Transformation and Social Change

Chapter 1

Discourse on education and social change

"Critical reflection may occur outside or within a discursive group. Discourse is understood as that special function of dialogue devoted to presenting and assessing the validity of reasons by critically examining the widest possible range of evidence and arguments in the context of attempting to find understanding and agreement on the justification of beliefs."

——Mezirow, 1998——

This chapter highlights the relationships between education and social change in Liberia. Chapter one also contains a brief discussion of the history of Liberia, the circumstances and underlying imperatives that led to its formation as initially a frontier society on the Atlantic coast of West Africa. I have elaborated to some extent on the broad theoretical outlines within which my discussion of a modus operandi for self-determination, social action and peaceful co-existence has been situated. I have also done a brief definition of key concepts in this chapter, which I would regard as central to my analysis for the benefit of readers who may not be familiar with the jargons of organizational learning and transformation theories. I will begin in this chapter by elaborating on the historical background of the Liberia society in terms of the unique circumstances of its birth as a nation on the West coast of Africa etc. I have also outlined and critically examined an array of motivational and cognitive theories that inform the mechanics of human action, self-determination, and personal transformation.

A brief history of Liberia

The geographically contiguous entity now known as Liberia has a past that dates back to antiquity thanks to the limited evidence provided by archaeological findings and oral traditions (Dunn and Holsoe, 1985). Anthropologists believe that Liberia's first inhabitants were hunter-gatherers, and ancestors of the Gola and Kissi peoples, both of whom form part of the Mel language group. These first inhabitants of the forest belt were presumably a part of a much larger group of Niger-Congo speaking people, which populates much of West Africa to this day (ibid).

The Gola and Kissi peoples were joined by the Kruan people (the Kuwaa, Bassa, Kran, and Dei ethnic groups) who were migrating from the north and east, and later, around the 15th century, by people of the Mende language group. Among this group were the Gio, Mano, Loma, Bandi, Mendi, and Kpelle (Tuttle, 2002). The main reasons responsible for migration from the savannah to the forest belt were associated with the collapse of the Mali Empire, and great population increases in the savannah. Migrant groups were also drawn to the coast because of the arrival of the Portuguese. In 1461, Seamen from Portugal began to call on the coast of West Africa, and this led to regular voyages and trade with the local inhabitants. In the wake of the arrival of Europeans, a new era of trade developed. The European traders bought gold, ivory, slaves, Malaguetta pepper etc., in exchange for iron tools, glass, and clothes.

Ex-slaves from the United States founded the modern republic known as Liberia in 1821. In 1820, the American Colonization Society (ACS) launched its first ship, the Elizabeth, which sailed with more than 80 African American emigrants. By 1827, slave states in North America took increased interest in getting rid of their free African-American populations (Cassell, 1983). This led to the organization of colonization societies in various states. These societies organized themselves independently of the ACS and founded their own colonies in Liberia for transplanting free African-American slaves. African-American emigrants were emancipated and recruited to join the colonization project only if they agreed to emigrate to Africa. The Maryland state colonization society established its colony in Cape Palmas, Liberia. Virginia and Mississippi also established Liberian colonies for former slaves and free blacks (ibid). See table 1.1 below for a description of the background and places of origins of the early black immigrants to Liberia.

Table 1.1 [Liberian Immigrants, 1822-1867]

Source	Number
American slaves emancipated to go to Liberia	5,957
Recaptured Africans	5,722
Free-born American Blacks	4,541
American Free Blacks settled in the Maryland Colonization Society	1,227
Other emancipated American Blacks	754
West Indians	346
American slaves who purchased their freedom	344
Other	68
Total	18,958

Source: Merran Frankel, Tribe and Class in Monrovia (New York: Oxford University press, 1964,p.6).

Beginning in 1816, Robert Finley, an American Presbyterian Clergyman, and the ACS began to address the problem posed by the existence of free blacks and manumitted slaves in "an America half-slave and half-free."

(Dunn and Holsoe, 1985,p.4). Many of the first arrivals died of tropical diseases to which they lacked immunity, and the group retreated to Freetown, Sierra Leone. In 1821 more settlers arrived on the west coast and founded a town at Mesurado Bay. Supported by the ACS and the American Military, in 1824 the settlers named their first settlement Monrovia, after U.S. President James Monroe, and the colony was named Liberia, from the Latin word *liber*, meaning free. On July 26,1847, the country declared its independence from the ACS. Joseph Jenkins Roberts was elected as its first president. Roberts spearheaded the founding of the University of Liberia, in Monrovia, and helped achieved the territorial expansion of the new country, most often through treaties with local ethnic groups. Liberia is one of only two African countries never colonized by European powers— Ethiopia is the other.

The republic of Liberia is located on the west coast of Africa. The country fronts the Atlantic Ocean for some 350 miles on the southwest and is bordered on the northwest by Sierra Leone, on the north by Guinea, and on the east by Cote d'voire. The administrative division of the modern Liberian state has evolved over more than 150 years of existence from dispersed indigenous communities, coastal settlement/hinterland regions, through counties/provinces, to ten counties with six territorial entities in the mid-1980s. Such divisions answer crucial questions about Liberia's history since its beginnings in the 1820s and its heritage prior to the 1820s. (ibid).

In current circumstances, the majority of the population is estimated to be members of some 16-28 ethnic groups, each belonging to one of three major language groups. These include the Kpelle, the Mano, the Bassa, the Grebo, the Kru, and the via. Traditional religions are practiced by about 70 percent of the people, while about 20 percent are Muslim and 10 percent are Christian. Almost half of the population is below the age of 15. The population growth rate in the capital and in coastal districts is relatively high and migration toward urban centers has always been vast, implying socio-economic problems such as high rate of unemployment and the lack of adequate avoidable housing. English is the official language, but African languages are used extensively. Far less numerous, but of great political importance in the past are descendents of freed American slaves (sometimes referred to as Americo-Liberians) who, as already indicated, were repatriated to Liberia to found this nation in the 19ᵗʰ century.

Overview of the Liberian education system

The modern educational system, like the political and institutional foundations of an emerging settler society in the 19ᵗʰ century, was founded by the ACS, and later, expanded by the colonial administration in the 1830s. The colonial government appointed a superintendent of education as early as the 1830s (Sawyer, 1992). Throughout the nineteenth century, foreign Christian missionaries played a leading role in the provision of education. For example, the Protestant Episcopal Church, which operated mainly in Cape Palmas, founded a secondary school at its Mount Vaughan Mission in 1850, the Orphan Asylum for Girls in 1855, and the Hoffman Institute in 1862. The Methodists also set up the Cape Palmas Seminary in 1857.

The education system, which was taking shape in the 19th century, was wholly inadequate to meet the scientific and technological requirements for future social and economic advancement. The core curriculum, which was being encouraged in schools, suffered from two major deficiencies (cited in Sawyer, 1992,p.120): learning was largely done by memorization; and the context of textbooks and other instructional materials were unsuitable for the African experience. These drawbacks in curriculum philosophy and organization have haunted the educational system up to present. The current educational system is characterized by various levels; Pre-primary and primary education in Liberia include kindergarten, preschool, and an elementary school for six years (Grades 1-6); secondary education includes three years of junior high school (Grades 7-9) and three years of senior high school (Grades 10-12); and the tertiary or higher education level comprise undergraduate and graduate university education and various subdegree courses.

The education system in Liberia has expanded from its very modest beginnings in the 19ᵗʰ century. As indicated earlier the tasks of educating Liberian youth were left exclusively to religious missions before the Second World War. However, the government assumed responsibility for all levels of education during the postwar period. Government expenditures on education had gradually expanded from $25,000 in 1900 to over $6 million in the mid-1960s (Lowenkopf, 1976). The United States also contributed tremendously to the expansion of education in the sixties (ibid). According to various estimates, the number of students in the school system (primary and secondary) varied approximately between 250,000 and 300,000 during the 1980s. About 60 percent of this figure is boys and the rest are girls.

School attendance has been historically lower on average for girls than boys, especially in rural areas. There are no exact enrollment estimates for the 1990s, but it can be surmised that these figures may have dropped considerably owing to protracted political and social upheavals, which began in 1989. The adult literacy rate was estimated in 1995 to be 38.3 percent—53.9 percent for men 15 years of age or older compared with 22.4 percent for adult women in the country. Higher educational institutions in the country include the University of Liberia[1] based in the capital Monrovia, Cuttington University College in Gbarnga, the W.S.Tubman Technical College in Maryland County, and the Teacher Training Institutions at Zorzor and Kakata.

The Ministry of Education is the official agency of the central government charged with the responsibility of planning and implementing educational policies. The Ministry of Education consists of three main departments: the Department of Administration, the Department of Instruction, and the Department of Planning and Development. The Bureau of General Supervision which falls under the Department of Instruction, is headed by an Assistant Minister whose responsibility is to provide administrative as well as instructional support services to all schools at all levels across the country. The country is divided into three main educational regions for administrative purposes. Each of these regions is headed by a Senior Regional Supervisor. Each

[1] The University of Liberia was established in 1862 as Liberia College. It is the oldest degree granting institution in West Africa. The University has trained many prominent leaders in the Liberia Society including leaders of state, church, commerce. During the colonial era in Africa, the University provided higher education for many Africans for whom education was unavailable in the colonies. This tradition continued in the postcolonial period (see Seyon, 1997,p.1).

county educational administration falls under the authority of a Chief Educational Officer assisted by District Educational Officers.

The Liberian educational system today is in complete disarray. As the economic basis to sustain political and social development has collapse, so have the educational infrastructure, material foundations and impulses for future growth. The ACS introduced formal or western education in the territory now called Liberia in 1831 when it passed a resolution to that effect. It has been more than 150 years since formal education was introduced in the country, and yet, Liberia ranks among the least literate of the English-Speaking African countries. The country has an average literacy rate of 30 percent and an annual growth rate in primary enrollment of 2.6 percent. It has been estimated that 40 percent of children of school going age entering primary education dropout before reaching grade one. Over time schools in Liberia have been gravely affected by high wastage rates (failure, repetition, dropout) at all levels. There has been a widespread need for qualified teachers, administrators, adequate financing and other vital facilities, such as school buildings and instructional resources.

As we gradually move deep into the 21st century, the need for educational reforms in Liberia has never been more critical especially in the face of the monumental challenges of national reconstruction. In an age of globalization and rapid technological change, the need to foster educational growth to cope with these epoch-making changes at the outset of a new century could never demand adequate attention. It is an understatement to emphasize that these fundamental changes require new thinking and perspectives and new ways of being in institutional and organizational systems. The changes ushered in by globalization also require structural changes in one's conception of the nature of fundamental educational goals and pathways to social empowerment.

One could speak of a form of interdependency between institutional adjustments and education—within the context of globalization, where human resources development seems to be the prime factor that more economically successful nations are capitalizing on. Thus the inspiration for this book arose out of an appreciation and understanding that one could make a tangible contribution to meeting these challenges—by fostering dialogue, rational discourse, social democracy, and new traditions and methods of criticalism. A process of all-inclusive and democratic governance has never fully gained ground in Liberian society since the formation of this republic in 1821 and this is one of our highest hurdles. Because of the absence of functioning civil and democratic institutions, a free full participation in dialogue has been anything but the rule as coercion and force have replaced critical discourses.

The absence of democratic and participatory discourse in framing policies for educational development has led to feeble attempts and haphazard measures to foster critical change in the education sector—a change that meets the challenge of globalization and rapid technological change in this modern era. It is suggested in this book that these historical norms, power and authority relations, and other forms of traditional barriers, have limited the scope for significant learning and meaningful transformations in meaning structures at the individual and social levels. The problems of educational underdevelopment in Liberia, then, can be identified in cultural and psychosocial assumptions, which have underpinned the process of institutional development and the absence of dominance free communication. This problem is also a profound reflection of the breakdowns of institutional practices. And it is the dynamics of these cultural and psychosocial assumptions that this study will attempt to illuminate.

Methodology and conceptual framework for social analysis

In light of the research goals and policy objectives of this study, I have selected to adopt an interpretative research methodology. This approach presupposes what is referred to broadly as a qualitative framework. Through the use of qualitative research techniques, I have been able to explore relevant themes, processes and patterns, which have characterized the inadequacies of educational policies and development interventions, and the impediments to social change in Liberia. These techniques are not coincidental. For, the overarching methodological framework forms the epistemological foundations of perspective transformation as an interpretive construct in the understanding of human cognition, action and personal transformation. Qualitative approaches and grounded research methodology tend to be predominant in the emergence of a developing paradigm that has attempted to capture processes of personal and social transformations.

The content of this book reflect a multiplicity of sources and intellectual ideas. Thus, I have also completed this book relying upon secondary sources in conjunction with primary and original sources. The secondary sources encapsulate major theoretical and empirical studies to explicate the categories of transformative learning and social action. Results of these theoretical and empirical studies have been reported in major adult education journals and handbooks including Adult Education Quarterly, Journal of Lifelong Learning, New Direction for Adult and Continuing Education—a publication in the Jossey-Bass adult and higher education series etc., I wish to indicate that an exploration of the social action and emancipatory dimensions of transformative learning theory, have underpinned the basic conceptual framework of this book.

Secondary data sources also come from the academic literature on education and policy analysis in Liberia and sub-Saharan Africa. Published material by bilateral and multilateral institutions forms an essential component of these sources. For example, these sources reflect work carried out by the World Bank, the United Nations Scientific and Cultural Organization, the International Monetary Fund, as well as individuals working in the name of these organizations. The primary and original sources will consist of official national and international statistics, newspaper articles on relevant subjects, as well as responses to interview instruments, which I have designed for the purpose of this book and previous studies. I have designed interview schedules for participant-observation research as a medium for critical reflection and improvement in practice; I will include responses to these questions to inform my analysis and conclusions throughout this book.

The interpretive paradigm, which is the governing principle of this study, falls under a broader perspective known as phenomenology. Over the years this phenomenological approach has broadened the scope of qualitative research approaches to focus on discourse and the development of interpretive understanding of social interaction—and this includes the educative process (see Mezirow, 1996). Phenomenologists drawing on the works of Husserl, Heideggar and others, see subject and object as one. The phenomenological perspective holds that prior to all description, analysis and scientific explanation, appeal must be made to a prior knowledge or prior understanding at the level of the 'phenomenal understanding' of the object. (Kortian,1980,p.62). This 'phenomenal knowledge' was later referred to by Dilthey as *verstehen* (understanding). The notion of prescientific understanding is what has been developed by Husserl and by Gadamer's exegesis of Heidegger's hermeneutic circle (cited in Kortain,1980). The phenomenological account of scientific method contests a constricted sense of experience as posited by the positivist conception of the human sciences. The phenomenological account of method is consistent with the epistemology of constructivism. The constructivist viewpoint argues that knowledge and reality do not have an objective or absolute value. That the knower interprets his/her reality based on his/her experiences and interactions with the external world. Glasersfeld (1995) reports that constructivism emphasizes the notion of viability as a test for judging the validity of social theories and models.

Phenomenologists contend that making a distinction between the experiencing agent (a researcher) and the object of experience (students in classroom or laboratory settings) is misleading. An adjunct to this methodological alternative is hermeneutics—the study of the meaning of texts. This interpretive tradition in the field of education has emphasized the context dependence of both measurement and the relationship between variables. Like positivism, phenomenology is a philosophy of knowledge that emphasizes direct observation of phenomena. Unlike positivism, however, phenomenology seeks to sense reality and to describe it in terms that reflect consciousness and human perception. Hence, phenomenology falls under the umbrella of the humanistic tradition— which emphasizes the common experience of all human beings and our ability to relate to the feelings of others (cited in Bernard, 1995).

The philosophical foundations of phenomenology were developed by Edmund Husserl (1859-1938), who argued that the scientific method, appropriate for the study of physical phenomena, was inappropriate for the study of human thought and action. Alfred Schutz elaborated Husserl's ideas. Schutz's version of phenomenology had a major impact in social science, particularly in psychology, but also in anthropology. The only way to understand social reality, Schutz maintained, was through the meanings that people give to that reality. The dichotomy between the two major epistemological strands pervades the social sciences. In psychology, for example, most research is in the positivistic tradition, while interpretaivism flourishes in clinical work. In sociology, there is a growing minority tradition of interpretive research, but the field is mostly dominated by the positivistic approach.

Semiology and ethnomethodology are significant methodological adjuncts to the phenomenological approach. Both approaches attach great significance to the fact that all meanings are contextually and situationally embedded. Ethnomethodolgists focus on the practices by which social actors make their actions meaningful in context (Misler, 1979; see also, Garfinkel, 1967). Garfinkel and Sacks have argued that the situativity of meaning suggests that all research should become the study of "remedying practices through which we make sense of each other" in the process of discourse and action (cited in Misler,1979,p.14).

Definition of terms

The following definitions have been aimed at covering some of the key operational terms used throughout this book. One cannot detract from the fact that the definitions provided in this section could be used in other contexts. However, the definitions outlined here are meant for the expressed purpose of reflecting the theoretical frameworks, objectives and analytical categories duly operationalized in this book.

Transformational learning

This study adopts the definition provided by Mezirow in his initial elaboration of transformative learning as a description of a cognitive process that pertains to adult learning and development (Mezirow, 1978). Thus, transformative learning has been defined as the process of perspective transformation. This is said to be the process of becoming critically aware of how and why our assumptions have come to constrain the way we perceive, understand and feel about our world, others and ourselves. The process of perspective transformation follows a learning circle initiated by a disorienting dilemma and resulting in a reintegration into society on the basis of conditions dictated by the new perspective. This process of critical discourse and consensual validation is an open-ended process because in transformation theory we arrive at a tentative best judgment until new arguments and perspectives are encountered (Mezirow, 1998) It has been emphasized that perspective transformation as a significant mode of adult learning allows us to strengthen our capacity for greater insight, agency, and self-determination through rational and undistorted discourse (Mezirow, 2000,p. xiv). I would direct readers for an extensive discussion of transformational learning in the section below on the review of theoretical perspectives.

Social action

The major goal of adult learning is to explicate the inner dynamics and structural features of an emancipatory praxis, which seeks to transform existing institutional and social order. Social action is the logical outcome of reflection, critical consciousness and rational discourse. Undistorted communication suggesting equal participation in discourse is a liberatory process that leads to participatory democracy and institutional change. John Dewey recognized this progressive function of education before the middle of the last century, when he envisioned using education as a means to foster social democracy in society (Mezirow, 1995). Mezirow (1997,p.61) has spelled out the connection between transformation theory and social action in the following terms:

> "Social activists educators can help learners to analyze their common problems through participatory research and the tactics of collective social action. The social action educator's role is limited…helping learners discover options for action and to anticipate consequences of these options by becoming familiar with previous efforts to bring about change, to building solidarity with others similarly oppressed; and to helping learners develop the confidence and the ability to work with others to take collective action, to interpret feedback on their efforts, to deal with adversity, and to learn tactics for dealing with the system…

Instrumental learning is a vital part of preparation for social action. The importance of learning new information and skills of taking social action is a crucial dimension for perspective transformation from an ethical point of view. Educators beware of placing learners in a vacuum by making them aware of the need for collective change without helping them acquire information and skills needed to implement it."

These critical observations are as pertinent to countries in transition, as they are to the realities of matured western democracies. Thus, social action in the Liberian context pertains to the achievability of power free communications and the taking of collective action to renegotiate State-Civil society relationships and create a democratic space for "dialogical voices". Invariably, it is these voices that will characterize the heralding of a new historic era of peace, tolerance, mutual respect, modernity, and unimpeded educational and social growth.

Perspectives for the 21st century

The new perspectives advocated in this book are based on the strength of the theoretical considerations and empirical findings of a variety of studies (Mezirow, 1978, 2000; Taylor, 2000). It is suggested that the ultimate outcome of this undertaking is to build a bridge to the future through a rigorous critique of the past and present. This assertion is predicated upon my argument that the anomalies of the past and present have led to a systematic distortion of participatory discourse and the preconditions for democratic practice. These new perspectives seek to reaffirm the inseparable connection between perspective transformation and social action. An essential component of this approach is to combine the imperatives of facilitating superior and integrative meaning perspectives with the praxis of transformative social action. Thus, the process of adult learning in organizational structures and the state system must become a process to achieve self-determination, a more critical awareness of one's role in society, and the recognition of collective and public interests. This is the central theme, which undergirds the perspectives for progressive social change in a new era in Liberia.

Review of theoretical perspectives

Over the years, various theories and conceptual paradigms have been advanced in the search for a generic theory to explain the underlying motivations for human action and behavior change in the arena of learning. In this context, a conceptual understanding has been posited by contemporary socio-constructivist theories of learning. Mezirow's theory of transformative learning in the sphere of adult education has been located within this constructivist tradition (Mezirow, 2000; Taylor, 1998). Hence, this recognition provides the logical basis for presenting a critical exposition of the inner logical structure of socio-constructivist theory, in an attempt to generate research questions and hypotheses that speak to the challenges of fostering new and dynamic ways of understanding, perceiving and interpreting the meaning of social realities in the Liberian society.

Socio-constructivist theories

Contemporary socio-constructivist instructional theory has posited a conceptual understanding that conflicts with early theories of human motivation. Pepper (1970) has described this early perspective as an organismic worldview. In such a perspective, the role of context is circumscribed to"facilitating or inhibiting"change, but not fundamentally altering its course (Hickey,1997,p.179). Allied to constructivism is the theory of situated cognition (Stein,1998).

This theory conceives knowledge and the learning process as a socio-cultural phenomenon rather than the acquisition of general information from a decontextualized body of knowledge (ibid, 1998). Thus, learning is essentially a matter of creating meaning from daily life experiences. As an instructional strategy, the theory of situated cognition has been viewed as a means of creating synergy between subject matter and the concerns and sensitivities of learners (ibid, 1998,p.1). Participants are allowed to use the raw materials of their experiences as a basis for creating knowledge. Socio-constructivist theories draw strongly from the theoretical works of Vygotsky and his followers (Cole and Bruner, 1971;Hickey, 1997). These theories essentially emphasize a contextualist viewpoint. From the socio-constructivist perspective, context has a fundamental role to play in the institution of the change process (Lerner and Kaufman et al as cited in Hickey, 1997,p.177).

Thus, radical socio-constructivism holds that motivation cannot be distinguished from the larger domain of activity, and the learning activity of the individual cannot be distinguished from the broader socio-cultural context of society (Hickey, ibid). It is this discussion of the individual as an autonomous entity, and the extent of contextual variables in determining the impulses for human action, that constitutes much of the debate in modern theories of learning, including Mezirow's theory of transformative learning. It is true that both contending theoretical orientations have contributed to elaborating various categories of thought, which explain the driving forces and nature of particular forms of social action, communication and cognition in the process of adult learning.

Theories of motivation and participation

Theories of motivation and human action have constituted the basis for developing a general theory of adult learning. And participation research has towered prominently in this scholarly enterprise. Much of this research on participation has been descriptive relying heavily on demographic variables (Pryor, 1990). Houle (1961) emphasizes three motivational orientations associated with high rates of participation. Based on Houle's findings, other researchers developed instruments to measure motivational orientations of adult learners. Bosheir for example, developed Bosheir's Education Participation Scale (E.P.S.), which has been used in several studies of thousands of learners (see Pryor, 1990). I suppose that it is quite possible to modify Bosheir's instrument to see how motivational orientations could reflect the willingness to participate in social action to transform historical and social conditions.

Fishbein and Ajzen (2003) have developed a theory of reasoned action. The theory was first formulated in 1967, but was revised in the 1980s to include the theory of planned behavior. The theory of reasoned action provides a framework to study attitudes toward behaviors. The most significant determinant of a person's behavior according to this theory is behavior intent. The theory holds that spouses, other family members, supervisors, and co-workers maybe referents whose inferred behavior expectations influence intentions to participate. The theory explains how behavioral intentions are formed. It demonstrates whether attitude or social pressure is more important in determining a specific intention. For example, single adults may be less influence by social pressure than married adults. Professionals in private practice may be less influence by social pressure than professionals employed in hierarchical organizations (ibid).

Around the 1960s, Harry Miller was one of several adult educators to tackle to problems of participation. Miller published a work in 1967 in which he hypothesized a link between socioeconomic status (SES) and participation in adult education programs.[2] Miller's deterministic social class theory was built on the needs hierarchy of Maslow (1957) and the force field analysis of Lewin (1947). Maslow had published a seminar work in which he posited a needs hierarchy approach. At the lowest rug of his needs hierarchy approach was the basic psychological needs, followed by needs of belonginess, esteem, aesthetics, and self-actualization.

Miller's basic strategy was to use the analytical construct of positive and negative forces operating in the external environment. Thus, in this particular context, Miller's participation theory could be termed as essentially a choice-theoretic perspective, placing the autonomous and self-directed individual at the center of the learning process (Hoffman, 1995). One of the major challenges in terms of participation in education and social change in Liberia is to identify ways to reduce the negative forces by rebuilding family networks and a viable employment sector, increasing incentives for education and democratic practices, thereby reducing the potential for civil unrest in society.

---

[2] Although Miller's research was conducted in the 1960s, but there is more recent empirical evidence to verify his claims. Recent statistical surveys, which include participation in adult education, tends to conform the hypothesis that there might indeed, exist some relationship between rates of participation and variables such as race/ethnicity and socioeconomic status (see US National Center for Education Statistics, 1995 Household Survey).

Darkenwald and his colleagues have extended Houle's approach by examining reasons adults give for not participating in adult education. Scanlan and Darkenwald(1984) and Darkenwald and Valentine (1985) used factor analytic approach to explore barriers to participation in adult education. These authors have identified six orthogonal factors as deterrents to participation; these factors include disengagement, lack of quality, family constraints, cost, lack of benefit and work constraints. Other scholars have combined the notions of barriers and motivators to participation in explanatory models (see Pryor, 1990,p.14). Rubenson (1971) expectancy-valence model starts with psychological theories of motivation, drawing heavily on the work of theorists such as Lewin, Tolman, McClelland, and Atkinson (see Cross,1981). The understanding that human behavior must be explained in terms of the interaction between the individual and his environment links the views of these authors. These views have also been reinforced by a theory of organizational learning as manifested through the dialogic structure of understanding (see Gadamer, 1979).

In Rubenson's model, the strength of the individual's behavior is determined by combining the negative and positive forces existing in the individual and the environment. Rubenson (1971) and Bosheir (1973) are quite explicit about the hypothesis that people with low self-esteem do not do well in achievement-oriented situations. This hypothesis is also implicit in Miller's social class analysis, where he considers lack of motivation a deterrent to the participation of people from lower socioeconomic classes (Cross, 1981). Bosheir's congruence model of non-participation of potential learners on the grounds that their low participation is due to the lack of congruence between their lives and the essentially middle-class educational environment of continuing education, constitutes a reaffirmation of an essentially social class oriented methodology.

Carl Rogers (1969)[3] has emphasized the self-actualization of the learner. Rogers has argued that the goal of education was to search for the realization of a fully functioning person. What Rogers is mainly

---

[3] Roger's theory of learning evolved as part of the humanistic education movement. His theory of experiential learning has influenced other theories of adult learning such as Knowles and Cross (see Patterson, 1973).

concern with is significant learning that leads to personal growth and development. Such learning process has five characteristics (cited in Merriam and Caffarella, 1991.p.113):

- Personal involvement
- Self-initiated
- Pervasive
- Evaluated by the learner

Personal involvement according to Rogers means the affective and cognitive aspects of a person who is involved in the learning process. The *self-initiated* characteristic is the sense of discovery that comes form within. The concept or characteristic called *Pervasive* signifies changes in behavior and attitudes as the result of learning. The characteristic called *evaluated by the learner* means when learners have the option to decide whether the learning experience is meeting a felt need. Knox has done research outlining the importance of change events such as getting a new job etc., as a reason for adult participation (Ralph et al, 1987). The issue of participation, to which the aforementioned authors have contributed variously, is one of the current lines of research, which is likely to constitute the foundation for future research efforts in the field of adult education. I am of the view that there are possibilities to modify and apply these theories of participation to an understanding of motivational orientations that lead to meaningful political and social action.

Motivation and self-determination

One of the most prolific contributors to the advancement of motivation theory is Edward Deci (Deci et al, 1991). Deci in collaboration with Ryan and Vallerand (1991) have advanced a self-determination theory of learning. This perspective seeks to promote in students an interest in learning, a valuing of education, and a confidence in their own capacities and attributes (ibid, 1991). The proponents of self-determination claim that most current theories of motivation fail to address the vital issue of energization. The model of self-determination addresses the critical issue of energization, by postulating about basic psychological needs that are inherent in human life. The theory highlights three such needs; these needs are competence, relatedness and autonomy.

A central pillar of self-determination is the assumption that social contexts that support people's being competent, autonomous and related will facilitate that motivated action's being self-determined rather than controlled (ibid, p.332-333). One can see how an understanding of self-determination in terms of patterns of authority relations in Liberia is significant to a theory of social and institutional change. Self-determination theory explicitly maintains that a non-controlling style of presentation in learning contexts has been shown to contribute to the internalization of regulation and to subsequent self-regulation (ibid, p.338). This view is akin to transformation theory, which claims that one of its underlying tenets is to achieve autonomy and self-determination through rational discourse (Mezirow and Associates, 2000, p.xiv). Howard (1989) has proposed an expectancy model of motivation, which seeks to transfer performance from the classroom to the learner's practical situation.

The author describes expectancy motivation as part of a dynamic process, which includes past experience, motivation, effort, performance, reward, and need satisfaction. I can see in Howard's analysis a theory of motivation, which has been further developed by Weiner (1986). Weiner (1986, p.12-13) has advocated a theory of motivation, which includes sequential or historical casual relations informed by nonparametric statistics such as causal modeling. Historical models of motivation include a conceptual schema in which expectancy leads to a particular behavior either directly or through value. And on the other hand, value leads to behavior either directly or through expectancy. In other words what we have are transformations of expectancy and value into specific modes of behavior via causal historical and sequential mechanisms.

McCombs (1991) and Wlodskowski (1999) have sought to emphasize the duality of internal and social mediation in the process of learning. McCombs reports that learning is a naturally active, volitional (see Deci, 1991), internally mediated and individual process of constructing meaning from information and experience. But McCombs has also intimated that learning is facilitated by social mediation in a variety of flexible, heterogeneous, and group settings. Wlodkowski has put forward a motivational framework, which suggests that human motivation is inseparable from culture. Wlodkowski argues that the tenets of his motivational framework reflect classroom strategies, which reinforce the socio-constructivist view of learning. Embedded in his essential motivational conditions is a variety of teaching strategies such as self-assessment, critical questioning and predicting, collaborative learning etc. Self-determination and self-regulation through intrinsic motivation is at the core of Wlodkowski's motivational framework.

In the early 1990s, McCombs (1990,p.118-119) summerized emerging psychological principles within which the relationship between motivation and lifelong learning would be clarified. These seven principles included the following:

Principle 1: Learning is naturally an active, volitional, internally mediated and individual process of constructing meaning from information and experience, filtered through each individual's unique perceptions, thoughts, and feelings.

Principle 2: Learning is facilitated by social mediation (interactions and communication with others) in a variety of flexible, heterogeneous (accross- age, culture, etc.), and cooperative group settings.

Principle 3: Beliefs and thoughts, resulting from prior learning experiences and based on unique interpretations of external experiences and messages, become each individual's separate reality or way of seeing life.

Principle 4: Thoughts and interpretations of external experiences and messages begin a cycle of cognition, affect, and reaction that serves to reinforce or support the initial thoughts(s) or cognitive belief structure.

Principle 5: In the absence of insecurity (e.g. feeling afraid, being self-conscious, feeling incompetent), individuals are natural learners and enjoy learning.

Principle 6: Self-esteem and motivation are heightened when individuals are in respectful, caring relationships with others who see their potentials, genuinely appreciate their unique talents, and unconditionally accept them as individuals.

Principle 7: Human behavior is basically motivated by needs for self-development and self-determination.

Self-regulated learning and self-determination are parallel terminologies used to describe learning strategies, which lead to confidence, diligence and resourcefulness (Wilson, 2004). Confidence, diligence and resourcefulness, in terms of how one tackles personal and social issues, may arise from critical reflection and transformation in meaning perspective. Linder and Harris (1993) outline six dimensions of self-regulated learning. These include epistemological beliefs, motivation, metacognition, learning strategies, contextual sensitivity and environmental utilization/control. These dimensions identify certain factors including; the will to learn and get better at learning, awareness of one's own thinking, identifying a problem and solving it etc.

Another contributor to the theory of motivation is Zimmerman (1990). He has identified characteristics of a student who is a self-regulated learner. These characteristics include; self-evaluation, self-monitoring, environmental structuring, organization and transformation, goal setting and planning, rehearsing, seeking social assistance etc. Attributional factors such as the amount of effort expended and judgments of task difficulty influence performance indirectly through self-efficacy (Bandura as cited in Schunk, 1991,p.211). Schunk (1991) views self-efficacy as the major determinant of one's ability to control one's own learning. Self-concept and self-esteem play an important role in enhancing self-efficacy. At the heart of these analyses are notions of the self and the role the self plays in the institution of belief systems, cognition, regulation, learning and change.

The cognitive process in dual societies

Anthropologists and cognitive psychologists (Dawson, 1967; Berry, 1976) have thrown light on the cognitive and affective variables, which help tremendously to explain the lack of progress in academic achievement in dual societies. My reference to duality as a constitutive variable suggests that in Liberia, you have a modern sector of education complemented by a traditional sector of education and socialization. These two sectors interact negatively or positively pending on the structure and nature of the interaction. One would argue that it is imperative to comprehend the nature and dynamics of this interaction in framing a model for cognitive transformation and social action. There now exists a body of literature, which seeks to explain cognitive processes in these dual and transitional societies.

Hvitfeldt (1986) reports that social theorists have attempted to explain cross-cultural differences in cognition by contrasting a modern "scientific" culture and a "traditional" culture. Horton (1967) has contended that in traditional cultures there is no developed awareness of alternatives, whereas in scientifically oriented cultures, such awareness is highly developed, as it is crucial for the development of science. Scribner and Cole (1981) tend to conform this thesis in their report of research among the via. They suggest that the differences may be due to the fact that "modern peoples" receive training in context-free communication while "traditional peoples" do not. Watkin, Peterson, Dyke, Goodenough[4] and Karp (1962) developed the concept of psychological differentiation or cognitive style using the field-dependent/field independent construct. A field-independent cognitive style is the tendency to rely primarily on internal referents in a self-consistent way, whereas, a field-dependent cognitive style is the tendency to give greater credit to external referents (Witkin et al as cited in Hvitfeldt, 1986).

Research done by Witkin and Goodenough (1977) has shown that field-independent people function more autonomously because of their reliance on internal referents. This allows them to structure situations on their own. What is clear to me, however, is that the collectivist solidarity and orientations of most traditional societies play a decisive role in the formation of psychological differentiation. Thus, Watkin and Goodenough (1977) have suggested that field-dependent people tend to seek more emotional ties with others and tend to have a more interpersonal orientation. Dawson (1967) has reported based on work carried out among the Temne and Mende tribes of Sierra Leone, that

[4] Ward Goodenough (1951, 1956) is one of the early scholars who contributed to the development of cognitive anthropology. He sought to establish a methodology for studying cultural systems. Goodenough's fundamental contribution has been in the area of componential or feature analysis.

such differences in psychological differentiation are often the result of child-rearing practices. His findings suggest that societies in which parents are extremely dominant tend to produce children who are more field-dependent, while societies in which parents play a less dominant role, encourage individual initiative, tend to produce children who are more field-independent.

Ramirez and Castaneda (1974) have reported that field-dependent people appear to be more successful with verbal tasks and content of human or social dimensions, while field-independent people tend to do best on analytic tasks based on inanimate and impersonal material. They referred to individuals who have the ability to cope with demands of both cultures as often as being bi-cognitive, functioning within both the field-dependent and the field-independent. Brookfield (1985) has argued that field independence is a learning style associated with open democracies, which encourage freedom and autonomy. Field dependence is characteristic of the learning conducted in societies with rigid social structures where authoritarian control is highly valued. This follows that field-independent learning style tends to favor the promotion of self-direction, single-mindedness and goal orientation.

However, some studies in the field of self-directed learning have pointed to the fact that successful self-directed learners exhibit characteristics closely associated with the field-dependent construct. This suggests that learning activities of successful self-directed learners may be located within the social context, especially when peers and fellow learners are cited as the most important learning resource (see Brookfield, 1985,p.9). Recent research has extended Piaget's concept of formal operations to emphasize adults' ability to reason contextually (Brookfield, forthcoming). The notion of post formal operations implies dialectical thinking, practical logic and practical intelligence (ibid).

Havitfeldt (1982) carried out a microethnographic study among the Hmong (the largest ethnic minority in Laos) in the United States and concluded that greater understanding of their cultural knowledge and the ways in which it influences classroom learning behavior can help in avoiding unfounded assumptions about how Hmong students perceive classroom interactions. There is not much evidence of this type of careful ethnographic study of how the cultural knowledge of Liberian students influences their cognitive styles and perceptions of classroom interactions. Even though there is no doubt that there is a need for such research to inform policy and intervention approaches. In fact since the 1960s, attempts to study teaching and learning practices from a cultural perspective have become frequent (Ogbu, 1992).

Stigler (1994) and various co-authors have demonstrated how the superior performance of Asian children in mathematics may be linked to roots in culture beliefs about the nature and origin of mathematics competence, as well as differences in concrete classroom practices. In his later works, Piaget paid great attention to the role of cultural and social factors in cognitive development (Husen and Postlethwaite, 1994). Piaget stated explicitly that culture is an important variable in cognition, although he never conducted an in depth examination of the link between culture and cognition. It was left to other authors to demonstrate that if the stage theory is examined in terms of processes of equilibration, the piagetian perspective "becomes consistent with a more contextualist understanding of human cognition." (Ibid, 1994,p.1245). At a UNICEF sponsored conference held in Sierra Leone, West Africa, in 1974, African Scholars outlines certain areas of research that needed further investigation, such as the area of concept development among African children (see Hale-Benson, 1982,p.24-26):

- To investigate the extent to which the mother tongue affects the learning of concepts in a new language.
- The effect of bilingualism and multilingualism on the development of concepts.
- The opportunities given for play and manipulative activities among children and the relationship of such activities to concept development.
- The extent to which African cosmology impacts the development of concepts etc.

John Gay and Michael Cole in their research on primary cultural differences (cited in Ogbu, 1992) reported that the arithmetic concepts in Kpelle culture were similar in some respects to those used in the western-type school but differ in other ways. The Kpelle had few geometrical concepts, and although they measured time, volume, and money, their culture lacked measurements of weight, area, speed, and temperature.

These differences in mathematical concepts and use had existed before the Kpelle were introduced to western-type schools. What is clear from the results of these studies is that cognitive attunement has an affective, as well as cognitive dimension, which facilitates or hampers adaptation (see Shade, 1989). Similarly, what the results of this study suggest is that the awareness of primary cultural differences must be incorporated in building viable instructional models that are at once formal and culturally particularistic.

In this context, many lessons can be learned from the apprenticeship system, which has long existed in vocational training in Liberia. The success of the apprenticeship system as a vocational program for adult learners, whether focus on tailoring or the acquisition of basic engineering skills, reflects the power of experience and reflective practice in a proactive pedagogical context. Because participants may lack elaborate language codes, they can start with experiential learning and move on gradually to building the intellectual capacity for extracting general principles from particular experiences. This process approximates to what goes on in formal classroom learning. The only difference is that participants in experiential learning must move from the field of action to symbolic learning or must combine both processes.

For example, Jean (1977) has argued that the inductive teaching/learning techniques of the tailor apprenticeship training do not necessarily prevent the formation of general problem solving principles taught as deductive techniques to enhance one's ability to problem solve on the basis of deductive principles. This notion solidifies the significant role of experience and reflective practice in developing competence and expertise for empowerment and social action.

Thus, in experiential learning the educational process is inextricably linked to the cultural contexts of learners and to their fundamental aspirations for social advancement (Daniel and Daniel, 1990). Furthermore, the main strengths of experiential learning or learning through practice are intrinsic motivation, direct relationship to further practice and less tendency to forget learning gained from action (Rippey, 1993). Commenting on the appraisive character of self-reflective learning, Mezirow has this to say (1985,p.25):

> "Knowledge gained through self-reflective learning is appraisive rather than prescriptive or designative. Action is emancipatory. The learner is presented with an alternative way of interpreting feelings and patterns of action; the old meaning scheme or perspective is reorganized to incorporate new insights; we come to see our experience better."

It is this understanding of appraisive learning, followed by corrective and emancipatory action, that forms the operational core and theoretical framework of my underlying theoretical posture. In this regard I will now turn to a discussion of Mezirow's theory of transformative learning and perspective change.

Transformation theory as a conceptual framework

Transformative learning as a theoretical construct was influenced by the concept of *paradigm*, made popular as a force in the historical evolution of scientific thought by Thomas Kuhn (Mezirow and Associates, 2000). A variety of other influences have been recorded, including the notion of conscientization, encapsulated in Paulo Freire's *Pedagogy of the Oppressed* (1970), the work of *Roger Gould* (1970) and the development of critical theory by the Frankfurt School of German philosophers and social critics. (ibid). Later, the critical theory of Jungen Habermas was a major influence on transformation theory. Habermas has differentiated three primary generic cognitive domains in which human interest generates knowledge (MacIsaac, 1996). These cognitive areas include work knowledge, practical knowledge and emancipatory knowledge. The work domain is known as instrumental action. Instrumental knowledge is based upon empirical investigation and governs by technical rules (ibid).

The practical domain or practical knowledge identifies human interaction or communicative action. In the domain of emancipatory knowledge, 'knowledge is gained by self-emancipation through reflection leading to a transformed consciousness' or transformation in meaning structures (ibid, p.1; see also Jarvis, 1987). Habermas places the processes of learning at the center of his critical investigation of postwar capitalist social organization. Welton (1995) reports that Habermas theoretical project signified a major shift within Western critical theory. Welton (ibid, p.26) has further stated in relation to the Pre-Habermasian pitfalls of critical theory that:

> "But there can be no doubt that critical theory's missing link until Habermas was its inability to link crisis and potential to a theory of how adult learning releases this potential in particular times and places, resulting in new institutionalized forms of freedom and enhanced individual and collective competence to be self-determining historical actors."

Commenting on the historic importance of Habermas's contribution to critical theory, Mezirow (1996,p.164) has this to say:

> "Habermas transcends both rational and the cognitive revolution by grounding understanding and learning in the very structure of human communication. We cannot make sense of the concepts of meaning, understanding, and interpretation unless we evaluate the validity claims (justifications) implicit in our speech acts: that what I say is intelligible, that its propositional content is true, that I am justified in saying it, and that I speak sincerely, without intent to deceive."

Transformation theory was first introduced in 1978 by Jack Mezirow. Mezirow's theory of perspective transformation is grounded in psychoanalytic theory. Grounded theory, an inductive theory building methodology, developed by Glaser and Strauss, is one of the sources of this theory of transformative learning (Merrian, 1989). Mezirow and his colleagues at Columbia University studied women in community college reentry programs and discovered that the central process of occurring in the personal development of women particularly in college reentry programs was one of perspective transformation (ibid). Mezirow's theory of perspective transformation is built on three major analytical categories—experience, critical reflection and rational discourse.[5] Experience is central to the concept of transformative learning. It is both the starting point and the content for critical reflection.

In transformational learning, experience is seen as socially constructed. Socially constructed experience can be deconstructed, acted on, and reconstructed (Merriam and Caffarella, 1999). In putting experience at the center of the learning process, Lindeman had earlier claimed that adult education was "a continuing process of evaluating experiences (Brookfield,1995).[6] In transformation theory, learners must engage in critical reflection to change meaning schemes and perspectives. Meaning schemes and meaning perspective constitute a frame of reference. Mezirow draws a distinction between meaning schemes and meaning perspectives. A meaning scheme is constituted by a cluster of feelings, specific beliefs, attitudes and value judgments that shape an interpretation. Meaning perspectives (habits of mind) consist of broad, generalized, orienting predispositions (Mezirow, 1996). Perspective transformation is said to be the process of becoming critically aware of how and why our assumptions have come to constrain the way we perceive, understand and feel about our world.

The process of transformation in one's habits of mind begins when we encounter experiences, often in an emotionally charged situation, that fail to fit our expectations and consequently lack meaning for us,

[5] Mezirow (1995) regards critical reflection as involving a critique of one's beliefs and understandings. Rational critical discourse is the means by which one participates thoughtfully and insightfully in participatory democracy. Meanwhile, Brookfield (2000) reports that critical reflection is a contested concept. The author outlines four traditions of criticality, which includes ideology critique, the psychoanalytically inclined tradition, analytic philosophy and logic and pragmatist constuctivism. Analytic philosophy describes critical reflection as a process by which one becomes more skillful in argument analysis (p.37). Constructivism rejects the appeals to universals and generalizable truths, and emphasizes the variability of how people make interpretations of their experiences.

[6] However, Brookfield (1995) has argued that experience should not be thought of as a neutral phenomenon. Some authors have observed that the way in which experience can be used in learning differs according to one's theoretical orientation (Merriam and Caffarella, 1995, p. 326).

or when we come across an anomaly that cannot be given coherence either by learning within existing schemes or by learning new schemes (Mezirow, 1991). In his earlier work, Mezirow (1978) identified ten phases of perspective transformation. Taylor has already reviewed studies regarding the empirical conformation of the phases of perspective transformation (see Taylor, 1997). I have conducted a micro-ethnographic study while facilitating an eight weeks college preparatory course at Jobs For Youth Inc. What I found to be problematic and less common among these participants was phase eight of the schema or stages of perspective transformation. Below is a table demonstrating the outcome of this study (see also appendences 1-3).

Clients' perceptions of the college preparatory program

Table 1.2   **Sample Size=21***

Clients' perceptions	Percentages (%)
This program has changed my views about going to college	98%
This program has helped to improve my self-esteem	100%
I have become much more open to others' points of view (stage 10)	20%
My understanding of college requirements has improved	100%
My overall experience with the college prep instructor has been positive	100%
I am able to critically reflect on my previous educational experience	70%
I have enough knowledge and skills that would enable me to implement my plans of going to college (**stage 8**)	60%
I am not afraid of trying on new roles	0.8%
I could relate to the concept and process of perspective transformation Before the instructor's explanation (0%) After the instructor's explanation (100%)	
The program has helped me a lot in becoming an independent learner	50%
This program has made me a little bit more reflective of all situations: By using critical thinking skills (20%) By using intuition (80%)	

*This sample included clients who spent 4-8 weeks in the college preparatory course. Students for this study were selected on the basis of purposive sampling.[7]

Kathleen King(1998) conducted research among adult students in higher education and found that 50 percent of them perceived themselves as having had perspective transformation. Mezirow's stage two of perspective transformation called critical self-examination of assumptions dominated the list of characteristics that were identified by the students. What this evidence does is to support the theory

[7] Like other methods of sampling, purposive sampling can be appropriate under given conditions. It can prove an invaluable methodology especially when backed by valid ethnographic data. (see Bernard, 1995).

that critical reflection is central to perspective transformation. Many of the ten stages of perspective transformation correlated with one another in this study. For example, 17 of the 44 pairs had a two-tailed .01 or .0001 level of significance (N=159). While most of the later stages (i.e., Stages 5,6,8,9,10) of perspective transformation correlated with each other significantly, the beginning stage (Stage 1) correlated with the earlier stages (i.e., Stages 3,4,5,6). The variation between the stages of perspective transformation in this study suggests that adults tend to group liked experiences when reflecting upon perspective transformation (ibid).

Experiences that lead to perspective transformation are often painful and stressful and can threaten the very essence of one's existence (Mezirow as cited in Taylor, 1998). Lobo, an American participant in a study conducted by Taylor on intercultural competence, described his change in perspective in response to living as a peace corps for two years in Honduras:

"I definitely see the world in a whole different light than how I look at the world before I left. Before I left the States there was another world out there. I knew it existed, but I didn't see what my connection to it was at all. You hear news reports going on in other countries, but I didn't understand how and what we did here in the States impacted on these people in Honduras, in South America, Africa, and Asia. Since I did not have a feeling for how our lives impacted their lives it was as if the U.S. were almost a self-contained little world. After going to Honduras I realized how much things we did in the States affected Hondurans, Costa Ricans. How we affected everyone else in the world. I no longer had this feeling the U.S. was here and everybody else was outside. I felt that the world definitely got much smaller. It got smaller in the sense of throwing a rock in the water creates ripples. I am the rock and the things I do here in the States affect people everywhere. I feel much more a part of the world than I do of the U.S. I criticize the U.S. much more now than I would have in the past (Taylor, 1993,p.175)."

Reflection is the central dynamic for learning in transformation theory. An ongoing process of critical reflection and rational discourse leads to significant learning, through the transformation of meaning structures. We may reflect on the content of a problem, the process of our problem solving or the premise upon which the problem is predicated. Sometimes reflection may be of a cursory nature while other times it may be deep, searching and profound.

Mezirow (1981,pp.12-13) has suggested seven levels of reflectivity:

1. Reflectivity: awareness of specific perception, meaning, or behavior.
2. Affective reflectivity: awareness of how the individual feels about what is being perceived, thought or acted upon.
3. Discriminant reflectivity: assessing the efficacy of perception, thought, action, and habit of doing things.
4. Judgmental reflectivity: making and becoming aware of value-judgments made.
5. Conceptual reflectivity: assessing the extent to which concepts employed are adequate for understanding and judging.
6. Psychic reflectivity: recognition of the habit of making percipient judgment on the basis of limited information.
7. Theoretical reflectivity: awareness of why one set of perspectives is more or less adequate to explain personal experience.

The first four forms of reflectivity refer to the level of consciousness "whereby people actually reflect upon their experiences (Jarvis, 1987,p.168). The last three forms of reflectivity Mezirow refers to as critical consciousness (ibid). Mezirow claims that conceptual, psychic, and theoretical forms of reflectivity represent a uniquely adult capacity (ibid). Content reflection and process reflection play a role in thoughtful action by allowing us to assess consciously what we know about taking the next step in a series of actions. Transformative learning is also the process of critical examination of problematic frames of reference that lead to the formation of new frames of reference that are more inclusive, discriminating, reflective and emotionally able to change (Marsick and Mezirow, 2002).

Critical reflection should be encouraged in professional training and continuing education in a post-conflict situation in Liberia. Critical reflection should form part of professional training of civil servants, teachers, educational leaders, union leaders and leaders of other civil society organizations etc. Fred and Associates (1998) have identified seven simple questions that learners can ask about a subject to enhance critical reflection:

1) Ask why something did or did not happen.
2) Ask what was good, why? What was bad, why? Neither good nor bad, but interesting, why?
3) Think of alternatives; what else could have happened? Why?
4) Look for other points of view.
5) Look for hidden assumptions in our attitudes and beliefs.
6) Look at something as a collection of parts (component) but also a set of qualities (values and judgments).
7) Ask who might be advantaged and who might be disadvantaged by these responses and actions.

Mezirow distinguishes between subjective reframing and objective reframing (Brookfield, 2000). Subjective reframing entails the critical self-reflection of assumptions. The possibility for objective reframing occurs when learners are doing a critical analysis of the concepts, feelings, beliefs or actions communicated to them by others (ibid, p.131). Subjective reframing is split into subcategories such as narrative, organizational, systemic etc. Systemic reframing is of particular interest in fostering an emancipatory paradigm because it involves critical reflection on one's assumptions pertaining to dependency relationships in the spheres of politics, economics, linguistic and other taken-for-granted cultural systems (ibid, p.132). The most cogent conclusion that can be made in terms of what transformation theory is, is encapsulated in Mezirow (1996,p.165):

> "Thus, transformation theory represents a dialectical synthesis of the objectivist learning assumptions of the rational tradition by incorporating the study of nomological regularities and the interpretive learning insights of the cognitive revolution by incorporating the concept of meaning structures, and a sensitivity to the importance of inclusion and interpretation of the

meaning of symbolic interaction. But transformation theory goes beyond the rational tradition and cognitive revolution to focus on a critically reflective emancipatory critique grounded in the very structures of intersubjective communicative competence. Through critical reflection, we become emancipated from communication that is distorted by cultural constraints on full free participation in discourse."

Mezirow further goes on to write (ibid):

"Searle's first three principles of the Western rational tradition pertain to reality construed through instrumental learning. Transformation theory supplements these principles by recognizing, through communicative learning, the salient but not exclusive role of language in construal, discourse, and reflective action."

The significance of rational discourse

Rational discourse is critical to the transformative learning process because it is seen as the medium through which transformation is fostered and developed. Discourse occurs when we enter into a "reflective assessment of validity"(Mezirow, 1985,p.19). This is a process whereby we "question the comprehensibility, truth, norms of appropriateness or authenticity of what is being asserted or to question the credibility of the person making the assertion (Mezirow, 1991,p.77).

Rational discourse rests upon a series of assumptions, such as understanding is derived by weighing evidence and measuring the insight and strength of supporting arguments, objectivity, that beliefs should contain no logical contradictions, the goal of achieving greater understanding etc. (Taylor, 2000,p.306; Mezirow,1995). Discourse, unlike everyday dialogue,[8] requires an interpretative stance necessary

---

[8] Mezirow (1985) distinguishes between the routine use of speech in daily life and the form of dialogue, which he refers to as discourse. In rational discourse, the validity of ideas is seen as problematic and hypothetical. The notion of change in perspective through discourse is also a central concept in Freire's theory of conscientization (Merriam, 1987).

to approach oral or written texts critically (ibid). The criteria by which an assumption is justified through discourse suggests the degree to which it is inclusive, permeable, differentiating and integrative of experience (ibid, p.54). Mezirow (1985,p.19) has lay down what he refers to as the ideal preconditions for rational discourse:

> "Ideally, participants in a discourse have full information about the matter at issue, they are able to reason argumentatively, they can reflect critically about assumptions and premises, and they have sufficient self-knowledge to assure that participation in discourse is free of self-deception. Participants in such discourse are free of constraint from coercion, and they enjoy full equality and reciprocity in assuming the various roles involved in the discourse."

Critical reflection, rationality and social context

Clark and Wilson (1991) have argued that a major anomaly in Mezirow's theory of transformative learning is his decontextualized analysis of experience. The two authors have proposed that Mezirow does not deny the existence of context, but what he fails to consider is the essential link between experience and the context "in which it arises and by which it is interpreted".(ibid,p.76).[9] Tenant, for example, reports that Mezirow does not give enough attention to the influences of social and historical forces and how they shape our lives, particularly concerning the social dimension of adult development (see Brenner,1991).

The main concern of the critics of transformation theory is that learning is conceptualized as a psychological process located within the individual, "giving primacy to human agency over social context".(Clark and Wilson,1991,p.79). This overemphasis on human agency and the

---

[9] In the 1970s and 1980s Labouvie-Vief's carried out work on adults' cognitive styles in which she emphasized how adults become aware of the critical importance of context. She argued that the major task of adulthood was to achieve cognitive subordination of "logic to social-system needs"(cited in Brookfield, 1988,p.323). One of the structural transitions of adulthood according to her was to achieve new integration in which initially decontextualized logic was to become "reembedded in its social context"(ibid).

psychology of learning is associated with the way the theoretical basis of the field of adult education has developed over the years (Imel,1999). Until recently, research in adult learning has been dominated by emphasis on the individual. This perspective views the learning process as an internal activity that can be governed by universal principles that can assist all learners, regardless of individual differences (ibid). But some authors have suggested that more work needs to be done to link the individualist viewpoint with contextualist perspectives, grounded in structural aspects of learning and a sociological framework (ibid).

Other critics have centered their attack on the claims that Mezirow's transformation theory is too rationally driven. Much of this criticism comes from depth psychology (Grabove,1997; Susan,1998). The goal of depth psychology is an expansion of consciousness or even a change in personality, rather than a cognitive change of a distorted frame of reference (ibid,p.92). This process requires a lost of ego control, and therefore cannot be planned. Scott (ibid) contends that grief is integral to transformation, whether that transfromative process is experienced rationally or extrarationally. Research activities in depth psychology seek to emphasize the mytho-poetic manifestations of transformative learning, by embracing adult learning and knowing as imaginative processes (see Dirkx, 2000).

For example, Robert Boyd (see Susan, 1998) has focused his analysis on the process of discernment in the transformation process. Discernment depends on extra-rational sources such as symbols, images, and archetypes to assist in creating meaning or a personal vision of what it means to be human (Cited in Susan, 1998). The process of discernment is composed of three activities, which include receptivity, recognition, and grieving. Grieving is considered by Boyd to be the most critical phase of the discernment process; it takes place when an individual realizes that the old ways and patterns of doing things are no longer feasible. It is the notion of discernment, which establishes the link between the rational and the extra-rational in the transformation process.

Mezirow (1991) responds to his critics by suggesting that adult learning involves the imaginative projection of value-laden symbolic models. These symbolic models are filtered through meaning perspectives.

And meaning perspectives are socially and culturally constructed; they may be shaped by social norms, cultural and linguistic codes or social ideologies, epistemic factors like learning styles, developmental stage perspectives etc. Furthermore, critical reflection and rational discourse are said to be manifestations of society's culture, and not outside of it. Thus, critical reflection, discourse and action can transformed "culturally assimilated assumptions and premises which limit and distort understanding and give learners greater control over their lives"(ibid, p.190).

In order to make transformation theory a significant theory of adult learning, the role of social and historical forces in shaping the lives of individuals must not be underplayed. As a significant theory of adult learning, and a tangible canon in critical discourse, notions of self-direction and autonomy of learners must not be emphasized at the expense of more complex and contested forms of identities, on the basis of psychoanalytic thought. Jarvis (1987) has concluded that experience and interpretation are social phenomena, so that sociological analyses are as important as psychological ones. Labouvie-Vief (cited in Merriam and Cafarella,1991,p.189) in studying the cognitive development of adults, has postulated that it may be the variables related to one's social context rather than age that account for particular developmental gradients in cognition.

John Dewey (See Rodgers,2002) views reflection as a systematic, disciplined and rigorous method of thinking which has roots in scientific inquiry. Dewey goes on to indicate that reflection happens in a community context, in interaction with other members of that community. In this communicative relationship the community serves as a testing ground for an individual's understanding, as such understanding moves from the private and personal realm to the public. At the heart of Dewey's conception of reflection is the rationale of creating a communicative space to facilitate individual and collective intellectual growth. Dewey's conception in terms of the primacy of dialogue as the basis for testing validity claims to one's conceptual understanding is similar to the logical core of transformation theory and Habermas' communicative rationality.

The social and cultural dimensions of adult development is particularly important for some countries impacted by dual systems of norms of appropriateness, tendencies of modernity, the forces of tradition, and normative belief systems. In these countries such as Liberia, multiple social and ethnic identities tend to be the norm. Social and historical forces in these societies may condition the persistence of contested forms of individual and communal identities. And the individual cannot, therefore, be separated from these apparent identities on the basis of the unitary self-imbedded in the psychoanalytic and rational tradition. Thus, this dichotomy of the individual and society must be transcended by an epistemology of intersubjectivity, action and critical transformation (Fleming, 2002,p.11). Indeed, the epigraph to this chapter reaffirms the cogency of these propositions.

It is in light of this historic and theoretical understanding that I have decided to probe into the institutional, cultural and psychological impediments; within the framework of historical and contemporary imperatives and challenges facing Liberian society. Indeed, questioning the legitimacy of historical norms and hegemonic power relations, with the expressed aim of anticipating social action on the basis of a superior meaning perspective, is at the heart of the educational project under most circumstances and socio-historical conditions.

What the review of the relevant literature demonstrates in this chapter is that there is a need to strengthen the relationship between transformative learning and social action, informed by phenomenological and case studies approaches (see Taylor,2000), to generate thick descriptions and reaffirm the generic character of perspective transformation. The task of research and praxis must be to combine personal and social concerns in transformative learning. Invariably, this is also my central objective in this book. I have explored ways through which personal transformation can be structurally and organically linked to social and institutional transformation.

Freire's conceptions of conscientization and empowerment suggest that personal empowerment and social transformation are inseparable processes (Merriam and Caffarella,1999). This attempt to explore how the theory of perspective transformation can be applied to the dynamics of adult learning in Liberia is also to demonstrate that the conditions of "ideal discourse", structural forces of cognitive change which lead to significant transformation in meaning structures, rationality, and emancipatory action are not a uniquely North American or Western phenomenon. Indeed, in late modernity, rationality as an operational concept is a commonality to all human cultures. And so are its categories of social thought, which reflect dialectical and historical contradictions in human society.

Chapter summary

This chapter has conducted a brief survey of Liberian history including the socio-historical circumstances that led to its birth as a nation state on the west coast of Africa in the 19th century. The chapter has also discussed an overview of the Liberian education system by highlighting its structure and the economic and institutional forces that have impeded its growth and development over time. This overview has amplified the need for structural changes and readjustments to facilitate the imperatives of decentralization within the system. The chapter has shed some light on the methodology and theoretical imperatives that have inspired my analysis throughout this book. The themes of transformational and organizational learning are elucidated with the goal of legitimating the aspirations for institutional and social change in Liberia. The chapter discussed transformation theory, its major theoretical sources and its categories such as critical reflection, ideal speech situations and reflective action.

I have agreed with Freire in this chapter that personal empowerment and social and institutional empowerment are inseparable processes, and therefore a theory of personal empowerment and self-determination must of necessity be a theory about social empowerment. What the review of theoretical perspectives demonstrate is that existing theories of human motivation to learn can be modified or extended to explain the causes or motivational orientations that have led to patterns of authority relations detrimental to self-determination and critical consciousness in a society impeded by specific psychosocial assumptions and norms of validation and belief systems. This assumption presupposes an interdisciplinary and holistic perspective that delicately integrates various social science disciplines to adequately explain patterns and causes of underdevelopment and institutional collapse in societies in transition, and of course that includes Liberia.

A number of hypothesis or research questions could be contemplated for further investigation within the framework of social change, and our discussion of existing theory and research above. Based upon a desire to facilitate more scientific investigations and deeper probing, it is plausible to pose the following research questions for further probing and intensive studies:

- What are the economic and cultural barriers to social action in Liberia?
- What is the role of constitutional change in pursuing social action in Liberia?
- How can traditional norms and cosmologies more generally contribute toward national reconciliation and social change?
- What are the economic and fiscal requirements for building a system of mass education in Liberia?

Chapter 2

Perspectives on education and emancipatory action in Liberia

"Others would add such learning is but the first step in recognizing that our most critical struggles are not ours alone, that major disruptions to our individual well-being are social in nature and require mutually agreed-upon strategies for change and collective action."

——Heaney, 2003——

The ideal conditions for public discourse in our society are the same as the conditions for elaborating an emancipatory praxis. Among these conditions are such cardinal principles, such as the equality of opportunity and freedom to participate in public discourse. Invariably, the democratic freedom to participate in public discourse also constitutes the platform for peace, solidarity and human understanding. Educational, political, economic, and cultural institutions and norms must be justified in terms of the ideal conditions of discourse and the potential for their realizations (Mezirow, 1985). The criteria of making value judgment constitutes the core of communicative learning and the interpretive epistemology.

Thus, the criteria of making value judgments, which in effect are the criteria of validating the ideal conditions of discourse, presuppose that cultural and historic norms and psychosocial assumptions are barriers, which must be overcome in fostering transformations and social action in Liberia. It is apparent to me that these barriers seem to be a commonality to virtually all existing historical societies often bedeviled by relations of dominance, class, race, ethnic and social differences. However, these barriers, as they may appear, often differ in varying degrees of complexity predicated upon the limitations imposed (or lack thereof) on individual liberty by the nature of authority relations in a particular society.

Students of African studies on both the right and left are in agreement that the highly centralized, postcolonial state in Africa is overbearing, restrictive, and predatory (cited in Sawyer, 1992). The overbearing state is noted for social penetration (ibid, 302). It attempts to exercise complete dominance over the levers of economic powers and civil society. The barriers to transformative learning in Liberia, then, are associated with the failure of a predatory and overbearing Liberian state, followed by a lack of appreciation of the historic significance of enduring dialogic processes such as culture learning circles[10] in forging a collective, self-governing authority relations, as an initial step to social transformation (see Jarvis,1987). However, this failure has its roots in the evolution of the Liberian social formation, which began in the early 19th century. More precisely, the historical imperatives of establishing a settler-dominated society, in conjunction with the influences of European Colonization of Africa are the predominant sources of proprietary state rule in Liberia (see Sawyer,1992).

[10] Freire has emphasized "critical transitivity" as the highest stage of critical consciousness. This stage is characterized by depth in the interpretation of problems, openness to revision and reconstruction, by receptivity to the new without rejecting the old, and by permeable dialogic forms of life (Freire, 1973).

Patterns of paternalism in Liberia

The evolution and consolidation of patronage, clientelism, and social and class cleavages in the Liberian society belie the high sounding principles and political ideals, which are said to have inspired the declaration of independence in 1847. The professed aims of the declaration of independence were to constitute a sovereignty that would guarantee to "all men certain inalienable rights; among these rights are life, liberty, and the right to acquire, possess, enjoy, and defend property." (cited in Dun and Tarr, 1986, p.44). But the challenges of social life within an alien environment combined with political and institutional inertia over the years, to produce an outcome that negated the professed aspirations advocated at the outset of nationhood. This aspiration was principally driven by the desire to build a Christian and Enlightened Black Civilization through the 'genius of self government'——among the "backward" inhabitants of the west African sub-region.[11] Commenting on the failure of settler society in Liberia, Basil Davison (1992, p.247) has made this cogent and critical observation:

> "In Liberia the perversion of community can be rationally explained as arising from the consequences of the slave trade. But alienation from ancestral community was then carried further, and systematized, by imposition of the culture of an imported oligarchy whose ignorance of local realities was easily encouraged, by the corruptions of power, into a contempt for the peoples who lived in these realities."

The changing contexts of party politics and the weaknesses of the institutional foundations of the state machinery have played a decisive role in the evolution of patronage.[12] Between 1822 and 1839, when

[11] There were two distinct goals envisioned in the repartriation plan of the American Colonization Society; the first goal was to establish an asylum for blacks that had suffered discrimination and degradation in the New World. The second and most ambitious one was to convert Africa into a garden of civilization and Christendom (see Gershoni, 1985).

[12] Christopher Clampham's work on the True Whig Party patronage system is insightful. See Christopher Clampham, 'The politics of failure: clientelism, political instability and national integration in Liberia and Sierra Leone', in C. Clapham, ed., Private Patronage and Power: Political Clientelism in the Modern State (London: Frances Printer, 1982), pp.76-92

various settlements were combined into a single micro-polity, there developed the beginnings of electoral politics featuring two main political parties; one representing the interests of an overwhelming commercial class based in Monrovia, and the other representing the interests of a more inland and coastal agricultural class (see Dunn and Tarr,1986). This political arrangement lasted for the duration of the Commonwealth period (1839-1847).

Between 1847 and 1877 partisan politics in Liberia took on a racial dimension. A mulatto commercial class controlled the echelons of power opposed by a predominantly black agricultural class. The republican party of the mulatto class remained in power until temporarily disrupted by the newly formed True Whig Party of the blacks in 1869. The rise of the True Whig Party in the 1870s was a response to the political aspirations of lower class elements within settler society (Sawyer,1986). However, the electoral victory of the True Whig Party in 1877 did not merely set out to correct the excesses of mulatto domination of an incipient political and institutional process.

This political confrontation led to a temporary crisis in the social order inaugurated by settler society. The crisis engulfed the founding fathers of the nation including Blyden, Alexander Crummel, E. J. Roye and others. Crummel denounced Roye's opponents in this political struggle as people who were opposed to the true spirit of the Black republic. In the eyes of Alexander Crummel, this spirit was undergirded by three central pillars—the goals of civilization, enlightenment and missions (Brown,1986,p.228). 1877 was the beginning of political consolidation in the face of the emergence of a new oligarchy; one that exercised complete domination and monopolization of power until it was dethroned by a military take over on April 12th 1980.

The dominance of sections of the settler population through the instrumentalities of the True Whig Party came at the expense of the vast majority of the general population—particularly the indigenous population. In the bipolar political arrangement [involving settler blacks and mulattoes] the indigenous population found themselves at the bottom of an unfolding social structure, with very minimal stake in governance and transactional relations. As the Lawyers committee (1986,p.12-13) has indicated:

"The years of settler rule were characterized by severe exploitation of the indigenous inhabitants, who still constitute more than 97 percent of Liberia's 2.1 million population. Half of the country's national income was enjoyed by less than five percent of the population. The ruling True Whig Party maintained a kind of feudal oligarchy, monopolizing political power and subjugating the largely peasant population with the help of the Liberian Frontier Force, an army of indigenous troops deployed to collect taxes and forcibly recruit laborers for public works projects. While the settlers along the coast developed an elaborate lifestyle reminiscent of the ante-bellum South—complete with top hats and morning coats and a society of Masons—the indigenous peoples in the hinterland endured poverty and neglect."

Thus, the indigenous population was subject to continual patronage, and in some instances overt mistreatment by all sides embroiled in this evolving political divide between socio-economic and racial groups in settler society. During this time, only a small number of indigenous children received education, those living close to Americo-Liberian settlements. Most of the indigenous population living in the hinterland did not get even a glimpse of Western education. The crisis between the central government and Christian missionaries in the 1870s led to the shortage of teachers, finance, and hindered the development of the educational system. Adjustments to this socio-political order were made apparent from time to time as was the case in the 1930s, when some indigenous leaders posed serious challenges to national authority and sought disengagement from the body politic (Sawyer, 1986).[13]

[13] In June of 1929 the United States State Department informed the Liberian authorities about a disturbing reports about the export of indigenous Liberian labor from Liberia to the Spanish Island of Fernando Po. The report claimed that the system of labor in question could not be distinguished from organized slave trade. The report further made mention of the fact that the Liberian Frontier Force, and the services of certain government officials were "constantly and systematically used."(Sundiata,1980,p.1). And the scandal began in the wake of this report that would involve the League of Nations and the international community. In the final outcome the Fernando Po labor crisis led to the forced resignation of President Charles D.B.King. This so-called "Native Question" in Liberia led to enormous strains in the relations between black nationalists and other advocates of black civil rights in America. Why some sought to justify the actions of the Liberian authorities in the forced labor case, and this include W.E.B. DuBois, other sought to denounce it as a betrayal of humanistic ideals

A decade after independence, Edward W. Blyden observed in an Independence Day address in 1857 "prosperity is not real, the prosperity of a nation is real when the springs of that prosperity are contained within itself, when its existence depends on its resources". Blyden went on to indicate, "I am afraid that the conditions which obtain between the whites and blacks in America are the same which obtain between us and our native brethren here. I am afraid too that as individual citizens we are throwing barriers in the way of assimilation and confederation which must necessarily take place between us and them" (see Lowenfopf, 1976).

From 1878 onwards a series of presidential successions took place within the framework of the True Whig Party. These presidents included for example, Anthony W. Gardner (1878-83), William D. Coleman (1896-1900), Charles D.B. King (1920-30) etc. President W. V. Tubman (1944-1971) was the longest serving president in Liberian history. Tubman ruled Liberia for twenty-seven years. He appropriated the excesses of the True Whig Party in his search to achieve a complete personalization of political power. Thus, the unlimited growth of an elaborate patronage machine and clientelism in the Liberian society saw its zenith during the twenty-seven long years of the Tubman administration. The essence of presidential leadership during periods leading up to the Tubman era and beyond was very clear as captured by Fahnbulleh (see Burrowes, 1989, p.41-42):

> "The role of the Liberian presidency was to ensure that the interests of the ruling Americo-Liberians were safeguarded first and foremost. All presidents of Liberia lived up to the requirements of the role, the most important attribute of which was to guarantee that what is good for the ruling class is good for Liberia. As long as the interests of this class were protected, the change in leadership was of secondary importance."

I have decided to devote the next section to explore the hallmarks of patronage and institutional decay under the Tubman administration. For, it is this patronage and institutional paralysis, which have become ossified through the decades, that have posed obstacles to undistorted communication, participatory democracy and social change. Before I proceed to the next section, I would argue that it has by now become perfectly clear that in order to remove these obstacles, the nation must come to terms with the imperatives of installing a new constitutional order based on dialogic approaches in policy formulations and in organizational and institutional systems throughout the fabric of our modern society.

The William V. S. Tubman Era (1944-1971)

President Tubman was born one of six children on November 29, 1895, in Harper City, Maryland County. His ancestors came from Georgia in the United States as freed slaves of Richard Tubman. Tubman received all his formal education in Liberia. After graduating from high school he read law under Monroe Cummings and Anthony Woods, and was admitted into the Maryland County bar in 1917 through the apprenticeship method——at this time law school did not exist in Liberia (see Wreh, 1976).

The Tubman era in Liberia signified the most vivid example of the personification of institutional and political power in the country. Tubman's inaugural address upon his ascension to power in 1944 reflected the critical issues that his regime had to contend with. Tubman announced that the spirit of his regime would be one of "No Reprisals; No Pay-Backs; No Get-Even With". He also indicated, "let the dead bury its dead." (cited in Lowenkopf, 1976,p.3).

The lingering suspicions that still existed among the various political factions, which prompted these declarations, included the slavery issue of the 1930s,[14] in which Tubman was indirectly implicated, and

[14] In a speech in the British House of Lords on April 25, 1934 Lord Lugard declared: "The Negro community in the United States appears to be misinformed regarding the true state of affairs in Liberia. We can understand and even sympathize with their desire to prove to the world that the Negro race is capable not only of self-government but of governing a subject people; but the fact Professor Johnson, an American Negro, was one of the Christy Commission, which exposed the slave-dealing and misrule, should show them that so far from establishing the prestige of the Negro race in the eyes of the world by championing the cause of the Liberian oligarchy, they are seriously injuring it (Lord Lugard as cited in Sundiata,1980).

the disappointing returns to Liberia from the Firestone rubber venture, "compared to the burden of the loan that accompanied it." (ibid; also see Wreh,1976). In addition, age-old geographical rivalries among coastal politicians had emerged during the contest for the presidency. The first prescription for strengthening the hegemony of the America-Liberian oligarchy was to infuse the population with new immigrants from the United States, the West Indies, and the British West African colonies.[15] This was also Tubman's first prescription for his approach to national integration and unification policy (Lowenkopf,1976).

After ascending to the presidency, Tubman packed the legislative branch of government with his servants, favorites, and cronies; many of whom were illiterate. Some chiefs, elected purely on the basis of Tubman's selection, had to use interpreters in following debates in order to translate from English, the official language, into their indigenous languages (ibid). Judges, Magistrates, Justices of the Peace and Traditional Chiefs, all owed their appointments to Tubman, the President. Tubman's wielding of power over the intelligentsia as demonstrated by his control of the University of Liberia, the nation's highest institution of learning, was absolute. Faculty and staff members were elected by the board of trustees on the basis of recommendations approved by Tubman. The board of trustees was often dominated by members of the legislative branch, most of whom as indicated earlier, were handpicked by President Tubman (ibid). Free political expression on the campus of the University of Liberia was "carefully guarded" as was the expression of dissent in the larger society (ibid, p.3).

President Tubman threatened to suppress any public sentiment that did not support his established orthodoxy on the most crucial issues—such as the economy, social policy etc. He had opposition party members removed from state employment and even private employment. These opposition activists could not get employment in any sector of the economy without his clearance. Unlike his predecessors, Tubman sought to become the unchallenged master of Liberia using a ruthless,

[15] In 1864 Edward W. Blyden, one of the architects of the Liberian Republic, wrote a letter to The American Colonization Society seeking its assistance to facilitate the resettlement of West Indian Blacks in Libeira to increase the "civilized population" in the country (see Lynch, 1978,p. 62-4).

firm hand and an iron fist. Institutions such as the Legislature and the Supreme Court—which were meant to provide checks and balances in the political system—were never allowed to pursue a path that was deemed inconsistent with the wishes of his administration. For example, Wreh (1976,p.23-24) has referred to a letter sent to a presiding Judge of a Civil Law Court by President Tubman regarding a decision rendered in a case involving the L. M. Ericsson Telephone Company and Mr. Arif Ghoussalny. That letter read as follows:

Figure 1.1 [Letter from President Tubman to the Civil Law Court]

——

Sir:

You are hereby commanded not to serve any write of executive or other relevant document emanating from the civil law court in an action between the L.M. Ericsson Telephone Company and Mrs. Arif Ghoussalny, until otherwise ordered by the Chief Executive.

Fail not at your peril.

> Given under my hands this 22nd Day
> of April A.D.1971
> William V.S. Tubman,
> **President of Liberia**

——

During the Tubman era the decision-making process in national government became his exclusive domain. Tubman was the most consummate micro-manager in this sense. To ensure complete control over institutional and social processes, President Tubman set up an elaborate security and patronage network. He set up the National Intelligence and Security Service, the National Bureau of Investigation, the Special Security System and the Executive Action Bureau. In addition, there was also the notorious Public Relations Officers (PROs). The PRO system was initially conceived as a social welfare and pension scheme to provide financial assistance to the less fortunate in society. But later this scheme degenerated into an institution, which would buttress the patronage system. The gainfully employed, the strong and healthy and others who preferred to live off someone else, were allowed to draw free checks from government largesse (ibid). PRO funds were also used to buy the support of opposition politicians to keep them loyal to the Tubman regime. The PRO system, like other dubious schemes undertaken by the Tubman regime, ended up depriving the nation of needed development funds.

Lowenkopf (1976) has divided the Tubman era into three main periods. The first period (1944-55) saw successful efforts by Tubman to supplant his old political enemies with individuals from both sides of the national ethnic divide loyal to him (see Sawyer,1986). The second period (1955-68) was the period of consolidation of the gains of a decade, which saw unprecedented foreign investment. The last period (1968-71), which ended at his death in 1971 was the period of retrenchment. This period was marked by diminishing returns in many spheres of national life, and a leader simply trying to hold on to power. Dunn and Tarr (1986) have broadly agreed with this historical taxonomy of crucial phases of the Tubman era.

The national bureaucracy was a mere patronage device under Tubman as it had been during previous regimes. Before the mid-60s as much as 40 percent of total government employment was disbursed outside budget channels. There was the notorious President Contingency Fund—from which the President disbursed monetary rewards to chiefs, party members, civil servants and other ostensibly needed causes. To the extent that the national bureaucracy was been used as a tool for personal political gratification, it could not be expected to serve as an engine of economic and political modernization. The economic impulses facilitated by the open door policy added an impetus to the expansion of Tubman's patronage machine thanks to the additional resources it made available. Stephen Ellis (1998,p. 158) in his description of the accentuation of the patronage system under Tubman has observed that :

> "Tubman's centralization of patronage combined with the great increase in revenue which resulted from the commercial alliances with foreign companies inherent in his open door economic policy to produce a political system in which the leader was seen as the personalization of the nation."

At the height of the patronage system, the typical government employee had a dual obligation. The government employee was obligated to the President and the True Whig Party as well. These obligations were carried out by attending political rallies of the True Whig Party, by voting for candidates selected by the President and Party, by public display of loyalty to the President, and by annual involuntary financial contribution to the True Whig Party. When President Tubman died in 1971, he was replaced by his then serving vice president— William R. Tolbert.

The Tolbert period was marked by unprecedented political ferment following an intense period of political patronage and paternalism during the previous regime. The growing political agitation on the part of hitherto disenchanted sections of Liberian society was a manifestation that longstanding dialectical contradictions within the patronage system had come to a head. Social classes that had long been ignored were becoming vocal in demanding new structurally organic systems of political discourse and a greater share in institutional processes. Sawyer (1986,p.2) has eloquently captured this growing political ferment in the decade of the 1970s:

> "During this period, the political pressure was all-inclusive and self-sustaining. For the first time in the political history of Liberia, peasant groups seeking more government outputs and/or greater opportunities for self-reliant development raised their voices around the country at the same time when government controlled union secretariats lost control of workers organizations which sought disaffiliation and self-rule at the plant level, when descending students founded student political parties, when the emergent Liberian entrepreneurial class developed an autonomy within the more cosmopolitan Chamber of Commerce, when the civil service itself sought aspects of a merit system, when market women sought greater control over the affairs of the urban market places, and the army of urban unemployed grew restless. These assertive groups covered a cross section of life in Liberia."

Many commentators and students of Liberian affairs have indicated that increased agitation by political movements, such as the Movement for Justice in Africa (MOJA) and the Progressive Alliance of Liberia (PAL) that later became the Progressive Peoples Party (PPP), hastened the demise of the Tolbert regime by fertilizing the soil for the usurpation of power by non-commission military officers on April 12th 1980 (see Sawyer,1986; Reno, 1995; Ellis,1998).

President Tolbert tried to liberalize the political system but was unwilling to go as far as was being demanded by an increasingly radicalized opposition clamoring for rapid structural and institutional change. The reason while Tolbert could not keep up with the pace of change in political consciousness was because Tolbert, like his predecessors, was born and bred in a value system and political culture that was not only allergic to change, but was ossified by historical and organizational norms that inhibited critically reflective learning and action. Because learning to think for oneself, and liberating oneself from our conditioned and taken-for-granted assumptions about the world, ourselves, and others is critical to making responsible moral decisions in a fast changing world (Mezirow, 1998).

Among the reasons for Tolbert's failures and perhaps the failures of most Liberian leaders is also the result of what Mezirow has come to refer to as systemic critical reflection of assumptions. This type of reflection involves critical reflection on one's assumptions pertaining to the linguistic, political, economic religious and other taken-for-granted cultural systems in society. Sirleaf (1999) has intimated that the Samuel Doe regime, which took over from President Tolbert and ushered in a new era of non Americo-Liberian rule in Liberia, could not meet the popular expectations of the people to formulate a vision for a country long in need of institutional and political change. This was because the coup leaders were essentially a product of the value system of the past and was unwilling to free themselves from the pathologies and psychological trappings of that past. What took place, then, was a passing of the guard from a tired and failed True Whig Party to a band of marauding soldiers who would unlashed havoc on all sections of society. Lacking coherent social, economic and educational policies, the Doe regime sought to rule by intimation, fear and the brute use of force.

The almost ten years of military rule saw one of the most horrendous abuses of personal liberty and political freedoms. The political liberalization, which began under Tolbert in the 1970s,[16] was torpedoed at the dawn of a new era—which began on April 12th 1980. Brutal military repression gradually took root as an institutionally legitimate mode of behavior in the decade of the 1980s. With the coming to power of Samuel Doe in 1980, the era of political rule though military force had begun in earnest. It was apparent that the country would never remain the same as the military sought to consolidate their rein using perilous methods. The military first embraced the populist movements, then the technocrats, and later sought a commonality of interests with disgraced fortune hunters and political opportunists (Sawyer, 1986).

Psychosocial and hegemonic assumptions

On December 24, 1989 some 100 insurgents claiming allegiance to the national patriotic front of Liberia attacked the border town of Nimba County from neighboring Cote d'Ivoire. This was the start of a destructive civil war that would last for seven years. More than 200,000 people lost there in fighting or massacres, and almost half of the country took temporary shelter in neighboring countries (Reno, 1998).[17] In July 1997, nationwide elections were held and Charles Taylor, the leader of the National Patriotic Front, emerged as winner, and thus became

---

[16] For example, there was a flowering of press freedom in the early 1970s, after the death of President Tubman. The early liberalism of President Tolbert resulted in the setting up of independent newspapers and magazines, including a popular newspaper at the University of Liberia called Revelation (cited in the lawyers committee for human rights, 1986).

[17] Reno has claimed that civil war in Liberia demonstrates a new logic of organization that has emerged against the background of the shifting priorities of foreign investors with the end of the Cold War and the collapse of the Soviet Empire. However, what is missing in this conceptual understanding is what role psychosocial and taken-for-granted conventional norms play in the predispositions, feelings and judgments of political actors and warlords. These presuppositions of mine are based on the fact that political actors and warlords, like every functioning adult, cannot be placed outside of the life circle characterized by developmental learning stages (see Mezirow, 1998).

president. These elections marked an end to the most destructive phase of the war (Ellis, 1998).

However, the elections presented a serious dilemma to the Liberian people. There was a stark choice between not choosing Mr. Taylor, and thereby continuing the war as he had implicitly threatened to do, or vying for an alternative political party, which would have restored genuine peace and stability. In addition, the results of the elections were also a demonstration of regional political exigencies. These exigencies led regional players in the Liberian peace initiative to opt for a compromised solution at all costs (Tiepoh, 2004).

Charles Taylor, as he had already demonstrated during the war, was more interested in building a personality cult like Tubman, then in building a moral platform for reconciliation and national reconstruction. The nation had encountered similar attitudes with Samuel Doe during the 1980s. After winning the 1997 elections, Taylor sought to establish a politico-military regime predicated upon oppression and the ruthless silencing of any attempt to question the conduct of national affairs. In late March 2001 the Anti-terrorist Unit and Special Operation Division (SOD), special units of the Liberian security forces stormed the university of Liberia campus to stop a peaceful rally. Dozens of students and professors were chased, hit with batons, kicked and flogged as they fled their classrooms to escape. At least 20 students were detained and held incommunicado for weeks without charge and several female students were allegedly raped in the aftermath of this incursion on the campus of the highest institution of learning in the country.

These actions were in conflict with Taylor's initial pronouncements, which were ostensibly to restore order to national life by liberating the masses from the tyrannical clutches of Samuel Doe. In the span of four years, however, Charles Taylor has proved to be one of the worst tyrants the country has ever known and perhaps—one of the worst tyrants in the checkered post-colonial history of the West African sub-region. I will spend the next portion of this section focusing on the numerous excesses of the Taylor regime. This regime bears all the hallmarks of a regime that seeks to limit the possibilities for institutional development and capacity building, to accommodate free full participation in dialogue and the reactivation of civil society, to become a dynamic force for change and modernity.

The obstacles to institutional growth under the Charles Taylor regime were catalogued in numerous human rights reports, books, Journal and magazine articles etc. One of the main problems of the Taylor regime was that there had never been any concerted effort to launch an enduring process or system of rehabilitation of former combatants. These are young men who committed terrible crimes during the war and still haunted by the traumas resulting from these tragic episodes.[18] In fact what the regime did against all logical considerations and the will of most reasonable people in the nation was to incorporate former combatants into a new security machine whose only purpose has been to instill fear in the general population ever since.

All the promises made by President Taylor to respect the freedom of free expression and other elementary freedoms guaranteed under the Liberian constitution were violated with contempt. Local and international human rights organizations as well the United States State Department added their voices and outrage regarding the suppression of press freedom in Liberia, and rightly so. Speaking at a conference hosted by the Association of Liberian Journalist in the Americas, US Assistant Secretary of State for Africa, Robert C. Perry, observed that (2002,p.1):

> "Because the United States remains a true friend of Liberia, we cannot, in good conscience, look the other way when we see serious injustices. As a result, and we strongly condemned the government of Liberia's April 29 banning of political activities, and we will continue to make our voice heard on developments within Liberia. In that spirit, we have appreciated similar protests from the committee to protect journalists (CPJ) Human Rights Watch, and others. In a May 6 letter to president

[18] When the National Patriotic Front fighters entered the Mandingo town of Bakedu in 1990, according to survivors, the fighters ordered all the Imams, elders, women and children to assemble in the town center. After the people had assembled, this forest-shielded town was immediately consumed by machine gun sounds indicating that women, children and elders had been killed (Kamara, 2000).

Taylor, CPJ sent a clear and direct message: "We urge you to ensure that independent media outlets are not harassed, and to allow Liberian journalists to practice their profession without fear of reprisal." I don't think we need to add to that request."

Press freedom is particularly important not only in terms of protecting the rights of the individual, but it also has strategic developmental implications. This means that free expression can be an important contributor to social development and the democratic growth of society. The freedom to express one's opinion regarding the course of public events in society is also important because of the fallibility of practical judgments. Classical scholars have long spoken to this foundational question as an important one in sustaining a democratic society. John Stuart Mill (cited in Rapaport, 1978,p.16) in his essay on liberty, emphasized the importance of free expression in a liberal democratic society in the following statements:

"But the peculiar evil of silencing the expression of an opinion is that it is robbing the human race, posterity as well as the existing generation—those who dissent from the opinion, still more than those who hold it. If the opinion is right, they are deprived of the opportunity of exchanging error for truth; if wrong, they lose, what is almost as great a benefit, the clearer perception and livelier impression of truth produced by its collision with error."

Hence, the political history of Liberia has shown that when alternative voices are silenced, and when the decision-making process is concentrated in few hands, in the face of fragile structures of authority, institutional power degenerates into personal power. Such process of transformation of institutional power into the personal power of the leader is often the corollary of economic and social underdevelopment. This has been the case in so many examples in Africa and the rest of the developing world. And this process is essentially what I am attempting to explain by examining it through the lenses of a cluster of theories and cognitive-developmental assumptions, regarding the nature and causes of institutional impediments in a developing society. In 1935 the Black Nationalist leader, Marcus Garvey, captured the excesses of political autocracy in the following poem titled Modern Man:

The men you meet are liars of the time,
As high as they may seem to you:
A statesman's ways are all sublime,
But ne'er a word of his is true.
The preacher talks for form alone,
And does like sinners bound for Hell:
To all these tricks the world is prone,
Although the Beadle rings his bell.
Between the State and Christian Church,
The poor are kept in their "good" place,
And if they kick, they'll be in lurch
With judge who stares them in the face.
It's God alone to save us all,
For not in man can any trust:
All mortals treat the rest like ball
They kick on field to yonder dust.
Next when your prayers you do say,
Ask God to come Himself to you:
For just as night comes after day
All men will prove to be untrue.
It may sound harsh to tell this tale,
But every man can vouch for it,
For he has had his timely sale
Of cruel conscience, bit by bit.

Marcus Garvey, 1935

Critically examining the nature and causes of institutional pathologies,[19] which can sometimes become dependency producing constraints as we have seen during the Tubman administration, and others following it,

[19] These institutional pathologies are embedded in meaning perspectives and political actions. Mezirow (1995,p.42-3) notes that a meaning perspective is an embodiment of a set of psychocultural assumptions, which are culturally assimilated for the most part, but also include intentionally learned theories. These meaning perspectives serve as codes that shape and delimit one's perception and cognition. Areas of cognition and perception include sociolinguistic (social norms, ideologies etc.) psychological (repressed memory, personality traits) and epistemic (cognitive and learning styles, focus on wholes and parts etc.).

and establishing the parameters of collective social action to eradicate them is one of the cardinal task of adult educators (Mezirow, 1985). This constitutes a cardinal element among the series of intellectual and analytical tasks I have set out to accomplish in this study. Brookshield (2000) has also referred to this type of cognitive examination and critical reflection as ideology critique. Ideology critique is critical reflection to uncover hegemonic assumptions, which over time become embedded in our consciousness as part of our every-day life and taken-for-granted conventional wisdoms. Guess (as cited in Mezirow, 1985,p.145) has identified this form of consciousness that produces dependency relationships as false consciousness. Gould (as cited in Mezirow, 1995,p.50) has identified "the search for hidden false assumptions of earlier developmental stages and overcoming their influence as the liberating transformative task of adult development."

In Liberia one might regard the overbearing nature of the state and the growth of clientelism as ideological forms of false consciousness. These falsely perceived forms of ideology and social practice have fostered dependency-producing relationships over the years, and buttressed the formation of the cult of presidential power embodied in an elaborate patronage machine, which in turn has constrained the growth of ethical norms as governing principles for transactional relations, institution building, and public consciousness. John Dewey (cited in Javis, 1987,p. p 169-170) elaborated the concept of miseducative experiences, which occur throughout adulthood, even into old age. These experiences occur in socio-cultural milieu and organizational systems in which individuals feel powerless to change the environment. Miseducative experiences lead to a "slowing down of thought and even the closing of the mind." (ibid, p.170). At the individual level, this is a world, which leads to an alienating experience and a process of self-estrangement as the taken-for-grantedness becomes oppressive (ibid). Removing these structural and cognitive impediments in today's realities is the challenge of social criticism, praxis, and concrete adult education work in Liberia in this new century. Stephen Brookfield (1985,p.47) is very instructive regarding this point:

"Endemic to this cognitive and affective change is the awareness that the world is not composed of fixed and unchallengeable givens or beliefs and conduct, but that it is malleable and open to continuous re-creation. Following from this awareness is the realization that individual circumstances can consciously be altered and that adults can, in concert with others, engage in a collective changing of cultural forms. Such forms comprise attitudinal sets, role expectations, stereotypical conventions and folkways, as well as social and economic structures."

Thus, the task of meaning construction in adulthood is to "validate competing assumptions through rational discourse to acquire more developmentally" superior meaning structures (ibid, p.51). This critical challenge also calls for strengthening civil society against what Habermas (See Inglis, 1997; Fleming 2002) calls colonization by the systematizing effects of the state, and placing the commitment to fostering critical reflection, critical learning and discursive understanding, at the center of national discourses and educational endeavors.

In this effort there must also be a commitment to reconstitute power relations in society. Michel Foucault concerned himself with the ways power influences the nature and ownership of knowledge. Foucault's analysis exposed the dynamics of power and manipulative structures in terms of how they interfere with the development of a progressive pedagogy "along lines envisaged" by the theory of communicative action (Collins, 1991,p.52-3). I will end this section by referring to Hart (1990, P.128) who has eloquently captured the civic essence of Habermas' idea of practical discourse:

> 'Within the framework of critical theory, practical discourse and critique refer precisely to the process of investigating and denouncing social and individual damages caused by power."

Perspective transformation and learning processes

The constituent elements of perspective transformation and social action are invariably embedded in the goals of fostering progressive adult education in Liberia. The goals of adult education are consistent with the universalist dimensions of a progressive tradition in the field of adult learning. This involves facilitating and nurturing self-direction, empowering adults so that they may see themselves as proactive individuals engaged in the re-creation of their personal and social circumstances (Brookfield, 1985).

To address Inglis (1997.p.6) fears of a "false sense of emancipation" in transformation theory, adult educators in Liberia would have to blend the relationship between perspective transformation and social action in their organization of instructional processes for adult learners. Learning must be organized in a way in which there is power free relations among all the participants. In transformational and social action education, learning must facilitate a critique of all forms of inequality and social domination, which persist in the greater society. Freire distinguishes between 'banking' concept of education and a dialogic form of education.

Banking education is said to domesticate students and reflects the hierarchical structure of dominance relationships in society. The banking concept is a negation of communal and collective forms of socialization, which persist in traditional societies. Concepts of field dependence in cognitive psychology are crucial to understanding dialogic and social action perspectives in these traditional societies (see chapter one). This point is important given the fact that Liberia is a typical dual society with western patterns of education and socialization on the one hand, and traditional constructs of learning and social practices on the other. In terms of the 'banking' method of pedagogy Freire wrote that (cited in Shor,1993,p.26) :

> "Education thus becomes an act of depositing, in which the students are the depositories and the teacher is the depositor. Instead of communicating, the teacher issues communiqués and makes deposits which the students patiently receive, memorize and repeat…In the banking concept of education, knowledge is a gift bestowed by those who consider themselves knowledgeable upon those whom they consider to know nothing… The more students work at storing the deposits entrusted to them, the less they develop the critical consciousness which would result from their intervention in the world as transformers of that world."

Freire has counterposed the traditional banking method with a dialogic and problem-posing method. In the problem-posing method, there is mutual search by both teachers and students to develop mutual intensions or co-intentionality, which creates a sense of shared ownership of the learning process. Thus, education for emancipation is a collective educational activity, which has as its primary goal social and political transformation (Inglis, 1997). Personal development is seen as an adjunct to this collective struggle to effect structural transformation. In explicating this notion that liberation is a social act, Freire has indicated that:

> "Liberation is a social act. Liberating education is a social process of illumination... Even when you individually feel yourself most free, if this feeling is not a social feeling, if you are not able to use your recent freedom to help others to be free by transforming the totality of society, then you are exercising only an individualistic attitude towards empowerment and freedom." (Freire as cited in Ingles, 1997,p.14).

This participatory process of learning is marked by thematic decoding of topical and problematic issues (Shor, 1993). The sense of shared ownership and democratic participation that develop in dialogic encounters helps both teachers and students overcome alienation in society (ibid). This dialogic encounter through critical reflection leads to critical consciousness, which is the same as perspective transformation as espoused by Mezirow (1990; 1995; 199; 2000) in his writings. Freire has described critical consciousness as having four basic qualities (see Shor, 1993,p.32-3).

These qualities are power awareness, critical literacy, desocialization and self-organization. Power awareness is knowing that society can be remade by human action and by organized groups in society. Power awareness also suggests awareness about who exercises dominant power in society. Critical literacy involves the creative application of meaning to social context. Desocialization is recognizing and challenging myths, values and language learned in mass culture (ibid). This quality of critical consciousness also involves critically examining regressive values, which have been internalized into consciousness—such as

63

sexism, tribalism, class bias, individualism and national chauvinism. The political aspect of this dialogic form of learning is manifested in classroom dynamics and in interpersonal relations between subjects in the wider society. This form of critical dialogue in the classroom and in an open society can be distorted by the hierarchical nature of authority relations and modes of socialization in society etc. Henry Giroux (1983) and Peter McLaren (1986) have written on this issue in their works. Paul Willis (1981) have also explored the phenomenon of student resistance to schooling in British working class communities.

The motivational dimension of transformations in meaning perspective is a crucial factor in dialogic encounters (Wildemeersch and Leirman,1988). Thus, the transformation process is based upon growing competence motivation, which is acquired in previous experiences. If there is no balance between need motivation and competence motivation, people involved in the transformation process will easily fall back on familiar frames of reference, which may no longer be suitable in the situations. This is while competence motivation is critical to eliminating feelings of dependency and lack of power in transactional dialogue (ibid, p.22-3).

David Bohm (2004) has set out three primary conditions for dialogue. Bohm holds that participants must suspend their assumptions to create common meaning in the process of dialogue. This assumption is very similar to Gadamar's notion of pre-judgments (ibid). The second condition involves participants viewing each other with respect and mutual reciprocity as colleagues and peers. The third condition calls for a facilitator who holds the context in dialogue. It is suggested that facilitators should never attempt to manipulate the process; their interventions should never be obtrusive. Bohm (2004,p.6) sees dialogue as a path to greater wisdom and learning:

> "Dialogue, as we are choosing to use the word, is a way of exploring the roots of the many crises that face humanity today. It enables inquiry into, and understanding of, the sorts of processes that fragment and interfere with real communication between individuals, nations and even different parts of the same organization. In our modern culture men and

women are able to interact with one another in many ways: they can sing, dance or play together with little difficulty but their ability to talk together about subjects that matter deeply to them seems invariably to lead to dispute, division and often violence. In our view this condition points to a deep and pervasive defect in the process of human thought."

Hans George Gadamer (1979) has made reference to the dialogic structure of understanding to demonstrate the essentially interactive nature of conversations and knowledge construction. In this context, Gadamer has described conversations as follows:

"[It] is a process of two people understanding each other. Thus it is a characteristic of every true conversation that each opens himself to the other person, truly accepts his point of view as worthy of consideration and gets a particular individual, but what he says. The thing that has to be grasped is the objective rightness or otherwise of his opinion, so that they can agree with each other on a subject." (Gadamer, 1979,p.347).

Critical dialogue and transformational learning as preludes to social action do not only take place in traditional classroom settings, they take place in private struggles, in the workplace, family settings and in self-directed learning groups such as study circles etc. (Dirkx, 1997). Following Habermas; Mezirow has suggested that the ideal process for structuring interaction is discourse (Kasl and Yorks, 2002). Mezirow (2000,pp.10-11) defines discourse as follows:

"Discourse, in the context of Transformation Theory, is that specialized use of dialogue devoted to searching for a common understanding and assessment of the justification of an interpretation and assessment of the justification of an interpretation or belief. This involves assessing reasons advanced by weighing the supporting evidence and arguments and by examining alternative perspectives. Reflective discourse involves a critical

> assessment of assumptions. It leads toward experience
> to arrive at a tentative best judgment."

Research in the fields of group and organizational learning has emphasized the merits of collaborative inquiry (Yorks and Marsick, 2000). Collaborative inquiry consists of reflection and action through which a group of co-inquirers seeks to find solutions to a problem of importance to them (ibid). The key notion of co-inquiry suggests that each participant, participating in this experience, plays an active part in the making and communication of meaning (ibid). Mezirow (2000,pp.7-8) has indicated that discourse is the primary means for developing more superior frames of reference, enabling learners to use the experience of others to assess reasons justifying their assumptions. In commenting on the same issue, Heron has intimated that valid meaning depends on the consensual view of its status and credentials. And that the personal views of reality one holds is interdependent with a public account (cited in Kasl and Yorks, 2002,p.6).

This suggests that the primary criterion of validity is congruence. And critical subjectivity is the process for achieving this criterion of congruence. Critical subjectivity also involves an awareness of the four ways of knowing, which are practical, prepositional, presentational and experiential (ibid). Kasl and York have argued that Mezirow's description of process reflection (see chapter two) is somewhat similar to Heron's critical subjectivity. Welton (1995,134) has suggested that the new social learning paradigm would construct the boundary of adult learning as wide as society itself. Meaning the whole of society will become a vast school. This boundary of adult learning in a learning society would include everything that constitutes the outlook, character, "and actions of communicative agents in space and time.

Welton has also intimated that this social learning approach assumes a number of factors: Firstly, the approach assumes that all institutions are formative in that they constrain or enable a reflective learning process; Secondly, social learning theory holds that an institution is miseducative if it is not a democratic learning community. In addition, it is suggested that in a democratic learning community, power relations and the asymmetrical distribution of dialogue chances and other structural forces, which distort communicative interaction must be constrained (Welton, 1995,p.134-5).

Social action is a cardinal dimension of the transformational learning process. Thus, problem-posing education is incomplete without a dimension that accommodates emancipatory action. Lindeman supports the view that "intelligence is consciousness in action—behavior with purpose" (cited in Heaney, 2003,p.12). He goes on to further assert that "every social action group should at the same time be an adult education group, and I go even so far as to believe that all successful adult education groups sooner or later become social action groups" (cited in ibid, p.10) Freire has made mentioned of the fact that authentic dialogue must lead to emancipatory action. On this issue he has cogently noted that (cited in Kidd and Kamer,1981,p.31):

> "Authentic dialogue must lead to action, which is then analyzed and evaluated before further action. Action is not just any action; it involves collective struggle to challenge the existing social relations which determines some of the basic components of social life, such as access to land, water and income."

The possibilities for dialogic encounters to have a healing and transformative effect in a society under constant strains of civil strife must be realized by placing these encounters at the center of everyday individual and group experiences. These everyday group experiences could take place in town hall and political meetings, county and student associations, labor unions, church encounters etc. As I have already indicated, critical dialogue or rational discourse, critical reflection and transformative action are the most important elements of perspective transformation. Rationality, and the ideal conditions of discourse or what Habermas (see Brookfield, 1993) calls ideal speech conditions and modernity are universal values. Thus, the ideal conditions of discourse and perspective transformation are the same in Liberia, as they exist in other societies.

But as I have already demonstrated in my previous analysis and claims, there is no empirical evidence to support a claim that such conditions have ever existed or if they exist at present in Liberia.[20] These conditions are inseparable from the creation of a modern educational system that lends credence to our understanding of the democratic nature of a viable public sphere. But as I have earlier indicated in the introductory chapter, the history of educational intervention in Liberia as a whole has been a checkered one. Efforts have been made to correct persisting problems in the system at various levels including organizational, planning, curricular and resource management.

But what has escaped these efforts is the need for a total overhaul and re-conceptualization of the educational mission in Liberia. Piece meal and haphazard approaches are not adequate in solving institutional and attitudinal constraints. What we have in Liberia is an educational system fashioned in the 19th century to serve the interests of a repatriate political elite, but yet many present day policy makers expect this system to be otherwise as such that it solves 21st century problems in educational and human resource development.

When the modern system of education in Liberia was being formed there was to attempt to reconcile elements of African tradition with the perceptual and operational tools of the Western system. This lack of recognition of the importance of incorporating the African experience in the dominant modes of socialization and training in settler society has already been mentioned in chapter one. A researcher made the following observation about a science class in a community school near Monrovia in the 1930s (cited in Sawyer, 1992,pp.120-121):

> "These little tribal Africans were being carefully instructed to eat plenty of beefsteak, baked potatoes, good fresh bread with pure butter, and to drink milk at least three times a day. The utter absurdity of this sort of thing is apparent when one considers that the African tribesman is lucky if he gets a piece of beef to eat once a year; that fresh cow's milk is unknown; that butter comes

---

[20] Although ideal conditions are seldom realized to become a part of human circumstances, what one can envision for Liberia is the existence of the most basic and optimal institutional conditions that embrace the practice of participatory discourse. This is a necessary condition for modernity and social progress as we proceed in this new century.

in tins a dollar a pound; that white bread, being made of imported flour, is confined to the residents of the Coast; and that white potatoes are imported from the Canary Islands or from Europe at an almost prohibitive price even for foreign residents."

Indeed, Alexander Crummell and Blyden, who were best friends and fellow workers in the beginnings of Liberia's modern system of education, largely shared (although Crummell's views were less subtle and sophisticated than Blyden's) the enthusiasm to supplant the traditional cultures of Africa in some distinct respects (Appiah, 1992). Blyden, like Crummell, believed that Africa's religions and political practices should be supplanted by the Western paradigm of Christianity and a constitutional order based on the values and ideals of republicanism (ibid). The conclusion one could make regarding Blyden's views about the project of civilization and education in Liberia is that it was much more complex, nuanced, and sometimes contradictory. While he showed great interest and worked toward integrating indigenous Liberian languages and traditions in the school curriculum, he was nevertheless, convinced that the project of repatriation was right and that perhaps it was the only means of "civilizing" the indigenes. In a letter written on October 22, 1885, to one Sir Samuel Rowe, then Governor of Sierra Leone, Blyden writes (see Lynch, 1978,p.353):

"In the Liberian territory where settlements exist, native wars are unknown. The natives find themselves in one way or another so dependent upon the colonists for such conveniences of civilized life as they value and for the training of their children, and so afraid of the superior weapons of war possessed by the newcomers that they are easily induced to settle their little difficulties."

Similar views regarding the role of Christianity in Western civilization and enlightenment could be attributed to Joseph Jenkins Roberts, one of the founding fathers of Liberia and its education (see Burrowes, 1998,p.39):

No, Mr.President. Unpalatable as the assertion may be to the calumniators of the African race, we would have them know they are made of the same material as ourselves. That the powers of faculties they possess are inherent in the African also and, although mentally prostrated, they are as susceptible of culture and can be brought to shine under the fostering hand of education as resplendently as their forefathers did when England had not yet beheld the genial rays of Christianity and when—enveloped in ignorance and darkness—her helpless sons were consigned to slavery. This, you know, sir, was once the condition of that now powerful and enlightened nation."

At a more general level one could argue that there was lack of systematic and sustained efforts in constructing a system of formal schooling. This was also the case in terms of the lack of serious attempts to construct a solid foundation for adult learning and education in the country, through cultural and literacy programs for example. The country did not actively engaged in a mass campaign against adult literacy until the 1940s, when the governments of Nigeria and Ghana began their adult education campaigns.

Dr. Frank Laubach was invited by the then Tubman administration to lay the groundwork for a national adult literacy program in Liberia. A presidential proclamation was issued for the commencement of a national literacy program in 1950. But this effort soon dissipated as with many other such efforts in the history of social and educational policy in Liberia. The adult education program that now exists in the country was perceived as an integral component of policies to induce rural development and agricultural self-sufficiency. There have been functional literacy classes organized under the rubric of the Community School Project concept. Currently there are also attempts to introduce literacy skills to ex-combatants as they gradually subject themselves to disarmament.

Community schools in the past were meant to provide basic education for youth and functional literacy classes for adults, as an initial first phase before the introduction of other nonformal education programs such as citizenship education, vocational training etc. But like other sectors of the educational system, adult education is in dire straits. The sector is suffering because of a lack of political interest in articulating a vision to nurture the progressive and transformative potential of adult learning. Problems afflicting this sector include a lack of strategic vision to ensure equitable distribution of educational inputs, lack of coordination of courses offered by various ministries and other agencies involved in adult and non formal education etc. International development assistance also played a crucial role in promoting basic and adult education in Liberia. Organizations such as the United Nations Scientific and Cultural Organizations (UNESCO) have a long track record of involvement in the field of adult and non formal education.[21] However, experiences of the past show that only internal structures are capable of playing a leading role in fashioning an adult education subsystem fit for a new era.

Distance education as an instrument of peace building and mass participation

Distance and community based learning are two important facets of the emergence of the system of mass education and the learning society in Liberia. Distance education, which involves the delivery of instruction when teachers and learners are separated in space and time, is currently being driven by microcomputers, the Internet and the World Wide Web (Imel, 1996). The convergence of new information technologies such as satellites, telecommunications, fiber optic technologies have made it easier for learning institutions to implement distance education (Darwa and Mazibuko, 2000). New distance learning universities and learning programs are being formed ever so often on the basis of the new possibilities in long distance communications created by the launching of new information technologies. Some of the largest universities in the world are distance learning universities. These universities include China Television University in Mainland China (530,000 students), Anadolu University in Turkey (578,000 students), University Terbuka in

---

[21] UNESCO's history of involvement in educational development in Liberia dates back to the 1950s. The organization supported the establishment of the Basic Education and Culture Center at Klay for pre- and in-service training programs of various categories of rural workers in Liberia. Ministry of Education staff have received various training oversees and targeted fellowships through the assistance of UNESCO (http://www.dakar.unesco.org).

Indonesia (353,000 students), Indira Ghandi National Open University in India (242,000 students), and Sukhothai University in Thailand (217,000 students). (ibid, p.9).

One of the main advantages of distance education is its cost-effectiveness. Studies have shown that distance education is more cost-effective than traditional programs, especially with large student enrolment and a solid support system (ibid, p.3). The most ambitious distance education initiative in Africa to date is the African Virtual University project. This is the first satellite-based program that will attempt to offer programs in university education and remedial instruction to students in sub-Saharan Africa at affordable prices. The new technologies and learning formats that have emerged have made it possible to design flexible programs and improve existing academic and vocational programs in ways that make learning fun for lifelong learners. In Liberia, the infrastructure for distance education is currently almost nonexistent.

The policy challenge, however, is to make optimal use of existing resources in galvanizing educational institutions to get involve in distance education. These resources, as meager as they may be, could serve as the beginnings for the development of effective distance learning systems throughout the country. There were about 70,000 televisions and 790,000 radios in Liberia in 1997. In 1999 the country had six FM radio stations and four short wave radio stations, while the number of television broadcast stations in the country in the year 2000 was two.

The independent media could hardly compete with the government and the ruling party that dominated this sector when Charles Taylor was in power. Thus, President Charles Taylor and his political party in effect owned the Liberia communication network. This was certainly a worrying situation when there should have been private media outlets to support non-governmental initiatives in the diffusion of knowledge. The communication network during the Taylor regime ran a television service, two FM stations and one short wave radio station; it had its own printing press, on which all privately owned newspaper had to be printed, and it published two newspapers. This is not doubt that some of these constraints have now been removed since the Taylor regime was thrown out of power.

The electronic media in the form of radio and television stations, as well as publishing houses, should serve as a focus for fostering comprehensive literacy and specialized programs through distance learning and education. But this can only happen if ownership of communication facilities and services are spread. There have been proposals to install various mobile radio stations, which may be currently on the international market. There are mobile radio stations with radiuses between 25km and 50km that cost about $4000 per unit. There are also solar power radios that have been widely used in South Africa and are currently on the market. These solar power radios I am told cost about $25 per unit. The technical mechanisms for considering these measures should be discussed in detail. (see Somah, 2004).

International institutions should be encouraged to assist the building of institutions for distance education, as they have already been involved in launching some distance education courses in the country. For example, in 2000 UNESCO was involved in collaboration with UNICEF and UNDP in developing distance learning program for Liberian teachers. These programs were to include sponsorship of a chair in the University of Liberia's Tubman Teachers College. In terms of community based informal education, study circles are vital facets of continuing education beyond the schools and college wards. They complement schooling and postsecondary education in a variety of ways. There is a need to encourage study circles in an effort to expand lifelong education, critical refection, and dialogue in what one might regard as natural settings of communities, in both rural and urban areas.

In this regard one could learn a great deal from the historical experience of the existence of study circles in Sweden. In fact I have learned from credible informants that study circles existed in Liberia among members of the youth wing of the Movement for Justice in Africa in the 1980s. But this was done on a very limited basis, and the entire exercise was an underground affair fearing retribution in a hostile political climate. Topics often discussed in these study circles were topical political and social issues of the day. The study circle movement in Sweden has attracted much attention, however (Oliver, 1987). Populist and democratic ideals decades ago inspired the movement. The duplication of the Swedish model has been encouraged in developing countries like Tanzania and technologically advanced countries like the United States. In a typical study circle, differences of professional and life experience are always regarded as a valuable asset. It is certainly worthwhile to study the Swedish experience carefully to see what lessons could be learned.

Chapter summary

What has been discussed in this chapter is that education and dialogical learning are important resources in terms of building emancipatory perspectives and practices. The chapter has also illustrated the impediments and limitations imposed on the growth of civil society because of the overbearing nature of the Liberian state. The chapter explored aspects of the historical evolution of paternalism and dominance relationships in the Liberian society dating back to political and cultural imperatives of an emerging nation in the 19th century.

I have concluded in this chapter that the failures of most Liberian regimes stem from specific patterns of critical reflection of assumptions, which have lead to inertia and institutional pathologies inimical to the aspirations for popular democracy and modernity. This inertial led to the emergence of worst forms of political autocracy in our contemporary era, such as the Samuel Doe regime followed by a merciless reign of terror imposed by Charles Taylor and his band of marauders and despots.

The chapter has discussed the notion of perspective transformation as a learning process that leads to critical consciousness and emancipatory action. The emphasis on dialogic encounters and their practical or technical dimensions such as competence motivation, the role of power in dialogue has been revealing. The most important aspect of personal transformation is the balance between need motivation and competence motivation. Competence motivation is critical to eliminating feelings of dependency and lack of power in dialogic transactions. Indeed, where competence motivation is offset by need motivation, people involved in the transformation process will easily fall back on familiar frames of reference. Hence, at the epistemic level, a theory of competence motivation is indispensable to a theory of personal and social transformation and democratic empowerment.

Part II: Education and Social Empowerment

Chapter 3

National reconstruction, leadership and school improvement

"Systemic critical reflection of assumptions involves critical reflection on one's assumptions pertaining to the economic, ecological, educational, political, religious, bureaucratic or other taken-for-granted cultural systems. We critically reflect on the canons, paradigms, or ideologies that have generated traditional roles and relationships, and how they have shaped and limited the development of our point of view and have fostered dependency relationships.

——Mezirow, 1998——

I will began part two of this book by discussing some of the major challenges that face a country in ruins. Everyone would recognize that in Liberia today, there is a dire and immediate need for national reconstruction and renewal in all vital spheres of society such as the economy, education, and historic interactions between the state and civil society. The need for national reconstruction arises out of the realization and necissity to rebuild a ravaged country and its institutions. Liberia has been classified as a war-torn country with a post-war population of 2.6 million and an annual population growth rate of 2.4 percent (World Bank, 1999). Other more recent estimates have put the population at 3.3 million (see United Nations, 2004). The war created nearly a million internally displaced (IDPs) and close to a million refugees, the smooth repatriation of which has tremendous implications for national reconstruction.

The economic picture in the immediate term seems very gloomy. A Panel of Experts commissioned by the United Nations Security Council recently concluded that about 1.7 million people in Liberia are in need of assistance. The study also concluded that 80 percent of people in the country currently live below the poverty line surviving on less than $1 per day. 35 percent of people were also found be undernourished while 75 percent had no access to clean water. Fewer than 100, 000 were registered as employed in the public and private sectors while 600,000-800,000 people were registered as employed in the informal sector of the economy (see United Nations, 2004).

Real domestic product per capita (PPP) has declined considerably to its current postwar levels of US$225m or perhaps even less. Nominal per capita gross domestic product (GDP) is estimated at US$188. In 2001 smallholder agriculture, which is the mainstay of the economy, manufacturing and services grew at a more moderate pace than in previous years. Today, it is estimated that less than 20 percent of arable land is under cultivation (ibid). Most of the country's socio-economic infrastructures have been decimated as the result of the 1989-1997 civil war and other subsequent conflicts. The country's human relationships were so badly damaged that once peaceful communities are now unwilling to live side by side as they did before the war. Repairing these relationships requires individual and collective transformations in our modes of behaviors and meaning structures, particularly in terms of the ways individuals perceive themselves and their relationships with significant others. This process of societal transformation really requires a rare spirit of solidarity and understanding never seen before in Liberia.

Thus, the process of national reconstruction essentially calls for participatory democracy through rational discourse and critically reflective action at all levels of the social system. Consequently, the main inspiration for this work has derived from an attempt to conceptualize the central features and character of such discourse and action, which must take place within the socio-cultural and normative framework of the Liberian society. Similarly, this book has presented data and a theoretical discussion in the previous chapters, which hopefully have addressed the central issues at the heart of this process of change. What can be concluded thus, is that the creation of new institutional forms that acknowledge the vitality of self-governing social forces is critical to dialogic encounters that ultimately lead to personal and social transformations.

I have endeavored in this chapter and throughout this book to provide a much broader framework that appreciates the fact that the role of various institutions (civil society, state, voluntary associations, workers unions etc.) within specific patterns of national discourses have tremendous implications for national reconstruction and institutional development. This follows that genuine reconstruction and energization of political and social life is impossible without a framework that nourishes grass-roots participation in national decision-making. It is the creation of this framework that should become the central historical mission and focus of educational projects and social learning processes in a new century and post-conflict situation.

The institutional framework for post-secondary education

The institutional frameworks for all levels of education and the articulation of these frameworks must be elaborated. The discussion in this book seeks to amply demonstrate that for Liberia to come of age as a viable nation-state, capable of solving its most pertinent developmental problems, all levels of education must be given a priority. The praxis of educational development and related research prove that dialogic forms of learning should become the foundations of new institutions that would ensure a path toward democratic development and social progress. Contrary to the views of Marcus Dahn (2001), I choose to argue that the changes, which must be made in the post-secondary educational sector, should be of a fundamental nature rather than the mere adoption of externally borrowed institutional forms and models.

Dahn, in a paper presented at a conference marking Liberia's Independence celebrations on July 26, 2001, proposed that the American Community College system might constitute a viable framework for solving Liberia's educational crisis. This proposition is said to arrive from the author's doctoral research project. While the American Community College system seems to posses useful qualities that might be worth duplicating in some educational systems around the world, it by no means presents a magic bullet for solving the most difficult types of problems that a developing country might face. Two-year associate degree granting institutions have long existed in Liberia such as the associate degree program in agriculture at Cuttington University College and other post-secondary commercial colleges in Monrovia.

In fact in recent years there have been a proliferation of associate degree granting colleges in the Monrovia area. What has been lacking among other things is the lack of proper coordination and linkages between various levels of the educational system. The current curriculum of post-secondary education also needs to reflect the unlimited potential of transformative learning processes. Furthermore, there are often cultural, historical and cognitive dimensions of learning that might not necessarily be adequately addressed through the mere adoption of a particular institutional arrangement such as the Community College system. Even in the United States, the Community College as an institutional framework has been designed to be of most help to only certain category of students. These students include those who might be most interested in post-school vocational training or others who might want to acquire basic skills in core subject areas.

Furthermore, the cost effectiveness of what a typical community college has to offer is by no means a universal phenomenon. In some instances, especially in cases of workplace training, it might prove more cost effective to train employees on site than referring them to community colleges. Providing onsite training for some employees might accentuate the essential problem solving nature of professional development. Thus, onsite training might help tremendously to breach the gap between theory and practice, thereby alleviating hindrances to the transfer of knowledge, which tends to be one of the most critical issues in professional development. Perhaps this is while small, medium and large companies across most industries are today more involved in the upgrading of the skills of their employees by investing heavily in workplace training and professional development programs. They see the comparative cost advantages and the quality of outcomes embedded in such corporate endeavors.

In the United States, brighter and more able students tend to enroll in four-year colleges. The community colleges have been designed to serve the needs of students in their local communities, especially those who often require academic enhancements and remedial programs to bring their academic and learning skills to levels comparable to those of their more able peers. The individualized and student-centered orientation of some community colleges also make them especially suited to fulfilling this function of remediation and intensive individualized tutoring.

Perhaps this is the reason why some school counselors and mentors might advice their less academically able clients to enroll at community colleges as an initial first step before eventually furthering their academic careers at four-year colleges. This way they might have the opportunity to improve their academic and learning skills before furthering their training at four-year colleges where the focus may not be so individualized and student-centered. I have had to tackle these issues first hand as an academic counselor for the past two years.

Furthermore, although there is general recognition that community colleges play a central role in providing occupational instruction for America's labor force, occupational programs at community colleges have been criticized for their narrow instructional focus (Perin, 2002). Perin argues that occupational programs at most community colleges are insufficiently concerned with literacy and critical thinking. The author calls for an integration of occupational and academic instruction to address these problems by breaching the gap between these two strands of personal development.

So, in various ways going to a two-year college in the United States can be a matter of convenience for some. For other students, especially for the more vocationally oriented, it might be because they want to pursue a middle level occupational and professional training at a two-year college. Still, for others, it might be because of the proximity and setting of such institution relative to their homes. What all these accounts testify to is that the two-year community college model as perceived for a particular purpose germane to American education may not necessarily be a panacea for solving the complex socio-economic and institutional crisis that have undermined the growth of literacy and professional education in Liberia.

The solution to the problem of academic underachievement in Liberia is far more profound than the mere transplantation of external institutional forms. Thus, the failure of educational policy in Liberia cannot be divorced from the enduring effects of the crisis of national leadership in education and the broader political sphere. National reconstruction calls for a platform for curricular innovations that embrace dialogue as a key to grassroots participation in shaping national institutions and the socio-economic life of society.

The lack of a strategic approach in designing educational programs that are consistent with the most immediate developmental needs demonstrates the absence of a clearer appreciation of the role of education in national reconstruction. Even in market-oriented economies where national planning has long been de-emphasized, there is often a strategic framework to enhance the development of human resources. There is a strong rationale for public action because the market for knowledge often fails (World Bank, 1988). The state is often therefore in a unique position to support efforts to breach the knowledge gaps by adopting policies for the development of a learning society. In developing countries where markets are relatively undeveloped, the case for rational state action is even stronger.

But in Liberia there have been no sustained and long-term commitment to develop education at all levels through deliberate and rational public action. This underscores the need to design and introduce new patterns of curricular, technological capability, and other basic infrastructures to accommodate a progressive vision for the future. The broader implications of the findings of this book as implied in my analysis and conclusions also demonstrate that these efforts should transcend mere institutional arrangements such as the duration of training at higher institutions of learning. Efforts at constructing the basis for a future learning society should incorporate the value of experiential orientations, and the primary cultural knowledge of those participating in educational programs in both formal and informal settings. A practical appreciation of primary cultural differences in terms of the relationship between the traditional sectors of learning and modern patterns of educational provision is necessary in boasting educational achievement. It is also a primary condition for building the platform for sustained engagement with the development and institution building process across socio-class and ethnic barriers.

The role of educational leadership

Educational leadership is significant in terms of institutional reforms and in implementing national priorities at the level of basic structural units. In Liberia, the challenges of educational leadership and national reconstruction are impossible to meet without the mediation of democratic dialogue and participatory decision-making. Educational leadership in Liberia should be accompanied by the tradition of critical discourse and social action— the fostering of which is the preoccupation of this study. This type of educational leadership, which might be referred to as enlightened and critical educational leadership, relies on the significant role of critical reflection in making sense of one's personal and professional experiences. This type of leadership is also crystallized in collaborative processes, where the decisions of individuals and micro collectivities carry the requisite moral and political weight.

The concept of instructional leadership, which emerged in the early 1980s, has substantiated the principle of collaborative and cooperative leadership. This pattern of leadership espouses exercising power through others, not over them (Conley and Goldman as cited in Lasway, 1995). Sergiovanni (as cited in Lashway, 1995) has reported that in a true school community, relationships are based on shared values, professional and moral authority, rather than bureaucratic authority. In the modern literature on educational administration, it is often emphasized that leadership is a managerial function that must be practiced by all members of staff.

The literature also underscores the point that management is "the act and science of achieving goals through people (Smith and Offerman, 1990,p.246). Allied to this concept of leadership are notions of strategic planning and participatory research, which involve the critical circle of reflection and action. This circle is indeed, the essence of transformative learning and emancipatory action. It essentially describes a problem solving perspective. It also fosters the identification and resolution of problem issues at the level of thought and practice on the basis of foresight and a democratic framework. This type of democratic educational leadership also requires a vision for not merely seeing what is, but foreseeing what could be (Heaney, 1993,p.18-20).

Standardized tests, school improvement and administrative competence

Nationwide standardized tests are annually administered in Liberia for students who have come to the end of their secondary education. This means that students who have reach grade 12th must take and pass the national examinations before qualifying for admissions in postsecondary institutions. These tests have been administered in the country since the formation of the West African Examinations Council to promote common standards across the West African sub-region. I have decided to discussed the results of the 2001 examinations in an effort to highlight the relevance of standardized tests to school improvement.

In Liberia the quest for school improvement is inexorably a quest for fostering professional education and lifelong learning. This recognition is based on the fact that there is a strong link between all levels of education— including primary, secondary, and postsecondary education in society. Highlighting a breakdown of the 2001 test results, even in the absence of available data to extrapolate long-term historical trends, does speak to a number of important issues in terms of how best to improve educational performance.

The 2001 national examinations results showed that slightly over half of all those who sat the exams did not make a successful pass. Hence, out of 8,049 candidates who sat the 2001 senior high school certification examination, only 65.7 percent made a successful pass, while 34.25 percent failed. Out of 18 schools, which had all their candidates passing, 12 were concentrated in the Monrovia. The remaining 6 schools were sparsely distributed across the rest of the country. Some schools such as St. Samuel high and Hannah B. Williams saw all their candidates failed while other schools saw all their candidates passed. Schools such as J.T. Dayrell Memorial in Maryland Country saw all their candidates passed. Several schools in Nimba County did not see any of their candidates passed at all. These schools include Garplay Inland Mission, Dolo Memorial high, Christian high, Kwendin Vocational Training Center etc. In Lofa County, only one school saw all their candidates passed. This may of course be the result of the disruption caused by the fighting in that part of the country.

One might pose the question as to why such a lopsided distribution of highly performing schools? One answer to this question might be the fact that there had been historically a higher concentration of high schools in the Monrovia area. And, therefore, this assertion would tend to account for the concentration of higher performing high schools in the Monrovia area versus the rest of the country. But such answer is insufficient from a policy perspective. From a policy perspective, a favorable distribution of high performing high schools across the country should be desirable. There is little doubt that a favorable distribution of high quality schools across the country is required. One reason for this requirement is the need to galvanize the citizenry for countrywide participation in processes of national reconstruction.

The process of national reconstruction involves not only the building of more secondary schools and resources to expand participation. While such an undertaking would be necessary and desirable, it is much more crucial to ensure adherence to a series of performance criteria derived partly from the lessons of high performing schools throughout the country. The 2001 examinations results could be used along with other tools as a diagnostic framework for guaranteeing good performance. A careful scrutiny of the national examinations results for example, can provide better signals in confronting a variety of problem issues. Such a careful analysis might provide some insight regarding real substantial differences between high schools throughout the country. There may be differences between schools on a number of crucial operational variables. And these differences to all intents and purposes determine academic achievement and school improvement in an era of reconstruction.

However, standardized tests are just one form of assessment, there are other ways of assessing students' achievement. There are also a multiplicity of factors, which influence school achievement and effectiveness. Deci and Associates (1991) have found that teachers' supports for competence (egg. positive feedback) will enhance motivation in general and may even enhance intrinsic motivation, if such supports are administered in a way that is autonomy supportive. Similarly, supports for relatedness (eg. the interpersonal involvement of parents and teachers) will enhance motivation in general and may enhance intrinsic motivation if such supports are also autonomy supportive (ibid). Research has also found that teachers' orientations influence the general classroom climates. Thus, students in classrooms with autonomy supportive teachers displayed more intrinsic motivation (self-motivation), perceived competence, and self-esteem than did students in classrooms with controlling teachers (ibid). What one can conclude from these research findings is that the extent to which the school context or environment is more autonomy supportive, rather than controlling, will determine the extent to which teachers will support the autonomy of their students.

Promoting best practices for educational and social change

There is little or no substantial and credible evidence of a concerted effort to create a new platform for educational development in Liberia. Readers would observe that these assertions amount to the overriding message in this book. This overwhelming lack of evidence of progress is the case today as it has been in the past. Educational development in Liberia has stalled on all fronts. Traces of failure can be found in the realms of practical policy and historic ideas. Similarly, the educational infrastructure is in complete disarray as the foundations of national economic life have long since evaporated. The national curriculum is inept and wholly inadequate for the aspirations of a modern society. In matters of practical policy and ideas, the lack of foresight has been particularly damaging. It has affected our actions and critical analyses in terms of creating a blue print for the future.

Thus, one must seek to offer a vision in terms of a road map for implementing radical changes for a better future. What is needed is a general precept of educational development that is at once historically concrete and specific. Such a general precept must seek to offer specific clues as to how best to revamp the educational infrastructure and underlying policy orientations. Such a general precept must also not only be limited to dwelling on the problems of the past and present, but it should seek to establish a framework for understanding much more intricate social and historical forces that will shape the future of our educational system.

Other techniques of learning and curriculum approaches must also be considered. For example, the value of experiential orientations in the educational process cannot be overemphasized especially in the arena of adult learning. The poignancy of this proposition is exemplified in the core tenets of Roger's theory of learning. Roger (1969) has argued that learning is most effective and facilitated when students participate completely in the learning process and has control over its nature and direction. Modern constructivist theories make reference to the vital role of cognitive structures in learning. What this essentially describes is how learners use cognitive structures by generating "rules" and "mental models" to make sense of their experience.

These theoretical premises are useful for understanding how students learn especially at the tertiary level. It is impossible to run a productive society in Liberia where more than 80% of the population are said to be illiterate. World Bank data shows that only 2.1% of the population currently participates in the labor force (World Bank, 2000). This figure must change through radical measures on the economic front if the country is to survive as a viable nation state in this new century. It must also change through an improvement in educational and training provisions to promote critical individual initiatives and entrepreneurship. There must be unity between a response to meet new economic challenges and general improvements in literacy and professional education.

In addition to high historical rates of illiteracy, there is today the alarming situation where most young adults, who because of their participation in the long years of war, missed out on the opportunity to acquire basic academic and learning skills in their early years. We now have an entire generation that has missed out completely on education in the country. To provide adequate programs that accommodate the aspirations of this cohort would suggests a radical approach suited to experiential forms of teaching and learning. What this case clearly testifies to is the need for a complex approach to a complex problem, requiring new approaches to institution building and instructional processes.

One of these approaches is the concept of a learning society embracing diverse approaches such as lifelong learning and distance education. Distance education today is proving to be more cost effective than other instructional formats (see chapter two). More needs to be done through national policies and multilateral efforts to improve existing technical capacity for upgrading and expanding the opportunities for mass participation in distance education programs. Of crucial importance here could be the setting up of an information technology fund to foster the growth of learning communities and the application of information and expert systems to solve complex economic and developmental problems.

The general lines of thought I have referred to should offer the epistemological foundations for not only a radical shift in policy orientations. But it must also offer the rationale for new and progressive forms of educational practice at the classroom level. I would like to suggest that these new forms of educational practice would have a lasting impact that will transform the educational landscape. These forms of educational practice would include the following features:

- Introducing strong quality assurance measures to ensure the cost effectiveness of educational provision across the spectrum. This would include monitoring teacher quality, the extent of parental and community involvement in education, student achievement, enrollment statistics etc. Such measures would eventually help to reduce waste and administrative inefficiencies in the system. It would also signal a more strategic approach to educational development and social improvement.

- Ensuring the diffusion of cooperative and experiential instructional methods at the tertiary level especially in adult education and professional development programs (see McCombs, 1991; Wlodkowski, 1991; Deci, 1991).

- Encouraging strong linkages between the demands of the economy and the type of curricula provided for schools and training institutions.

- And finally, developing the infrastructure for the widespread use of computer-based learning models to remove the knowledge gap between various students at schools and colleges. Resources mobilized through the information technology fund could be deployed to fulfill this task.

This section has elaborated on some of the crucial features of the sort of best practices that must be encouraged for a new type of education to become part of our policy thinking and practices. This new type of education in a nutshell calls for the combination of building new institutional organizations and encouraging the adoption of progressive and modern classroom methods. The ideas proposed in this section are by no means novel but they can be made historically and politically pertinent to the realities of educational development in Liberia. For even if the current state of affairs in society is as such that education has been completely neglected, hopefully, and sooner or later, the stage will be set for a new epoch of progressive development that will call on our sense of civic duty and vocation to uplift humanity through education and critical consciousness.

Chapter Summary

This chapter has emphasized the need for a interlocking process of national reconstruction that affect all spheres including the political, social, economic and the demands of modernization of the education system. What I have argued in this chapter is that the failure of educational policy over the years is a broader reflection of a deep seated and systemic crisis of national leadership. The crisis must be addressed as a matter of first priority. A distinguishing feature of this leadership failure is the lack of foresight and strategic planning to anticipate educational and social change. The chapter has concluded that ultimately the demands of a new economy must be reflected in new patterns of curricula construction and design so that there is logical correspondence between the educational process and the system of political economy.

This chapter concludes that part of the process of institution building will include leadership training, effective school leadership and management and decentralization of decision-making. The process of decentralization of decision-making in the educational sector could include electing district educational officers or school boards to administer education, particularly in the counties and other sub-divisions. The chapter has also concluded that more creative ways to reduce waste, corruption and the infusion of best practices through such instruments as revamped national examinations and other appropriate diagnostic tools must be contemplated through national policy.

Chapter 4

Education, civil society and social empowerment

"Many different interpretations of critique and critical reflection are possible, with different purposes, and involving different procedures. From the perspective of emancipatory education, however, the meaning of critique is inseparably linked to questioning those norms, which stabilize relations of force. Critique can therefore take place only in the medium of communicative action."

—Hart, 1990—

I would begin this chapter by drawing attention to Jungen Habermas' crucial distinctions between instrumental and communicative actions.

Unlike Marx, Habermas maintains that communicative action and competence cannot be achieved directly through productive activity, but through the critical and revolutionary activity of social forces or what he calls the "struggling classes." Rational criticism and self-determination can be achieved only in conditions of communicative action or power free discourse. Thus, Habermas (1987, p.8) has indicated that:

> "While instrumental action corresponds to the constraint of external nature and the level of the forces of production determines the extent of technical control over natural forces, communicative action stands in correspondence to the suppression of man's own nature. The institutional framework determines the extent of repression by the unreflected, "natural" forces of social dependence and political power, which is rooted in prior history and tradition. A society owes emancipation from the external forces of nature to labor processes, that is to the production of technically exploitable knowledge (including "the transformation, of natural sciences into machinery"). Emancipation from compulsion of internal nature succeeds to the degree that institutions based on force are replaced by an organization of social relations that is bound only to communication free from domination."

This chapter is composed of a collection of various essays that have highlighted the relationship between education, civil society and social learning. The chapter underscores the vital role of education and dialogic forms of learning in galvanizing citizens for civic action. I have also discussed patterns of civil organization and emphasized as I have done throughout this book, that the attainment of critical consciousness is both a practical and humanistic goal in the process of personal and social transformation in Liberian society. I will look at cultural and symbolic dimensions of civil society as determining the parameters for action-orienting norms and value systems within the spirit of Gramcian social thought and methodology. The chapter has been divided into four sections. These sections duly elaborate upon issues and themes that are at the core of the vital role of communication, critique, and critical consciousness in the reconstitution of social order in the Liberian society after decades of drift and institutional paralysis.

I
Education and civil society in Liberia

Education and learning are very critical to the building and strengthening of a vibrant civil society especially in a society that is recovering from a prolonged period of conflict. One might note that the question regarding the role of education and learning in civil society is not a new one. Indeed, it has been raised many times before. Structural Functionalist theorists, working in the field of the sociology of education, and scholars of other methodological and theoretical leanings, have commented variously on this issue (see Parsons, 1951, 1967; Turner, 1991; Knapp, 1994). I would argue that through social learning and critical reflection as posited in this book, we are often empowered to learn the great lessons of history. Learning the great lessons of history so that the most unpleasant historical experiences may not be repeated, even under the most challenging and tedious conditions, is significant to our conceptions of education and civil society from a means-ends perspective.

However, it is suggested here that only a specific kind of educational goals can facilitate transactional relations within the spheres of civil society, such as the formation of a viable civic community and democratic culture. This suggestion invariably embraces the most ambitious and overarching framework for social change, which should be reflected in the conception of the new educational challenge and goals. This basic operational framework and understanding of social change enables participation, dialogue and the finest intuitive impulses imbedded within a given civil society, and sometimes even within the domain of a duly constituted democratic state. These impulses and progressive orientations are those of solidarity, a sense of shared historical destiny and cultural values, symbolized in one's willingness to sacrifice in the interest of the community. These value orientations should further define and delimit discourse and the parameters of our engagement in the historical process. They must therefore inform our basic normative orientations in the general scheme of things and in the onward march to modernity and a culture of freedom and social justice.

I believe that the framework within which education can lead to strengthening civil society as a sphere of interpretive discourse must be built upon an appreciation of the magnitude and urgency of socio-historical change in a conflict ridden and criminalized Liberian society. After more than a century and a half of national existence, the urgency of social change must not be perceived as a matter of political expediency as politicians are often tempted to do. There are dire and substantial consequences involved if the status quo remains the same. The reasons for change are too important to be treated in a cavalier fashion.

For, the superficiality of political actions, which is often the offshoot of misguided social consciousness and intensions, would be simply counterintuitive at this juncture. What is imperative, however, is that this unique challenge, which requires overarching structural adaptations and change in our psychosocial assumptions and other forms of national consciousness, be understood as being intimately linked to the survival of the nation state, now, and in the near future. The structural and institutional adaptations I am referring to must be invariably located within the context of a dynamic relationship between education, civil society and state institutions: A relationship based on dialogue, understanding, critical reflection and social change.

A metaphor for defining civil society

Civil society is described as a cite of social power as opposed to the state, which is the main seat of political authoritative power (see Bashiriyeh, 2004). Political thought in the 18th and 19th century conceptualized the distinctions between the state and civil society. The early roots of civil society, at least in Europe, can be traced back to feudal society in the Middle Ages. In contrast to the West, in Eastern societies, oriental despotism and the Asiatic mode of production acted as structural impediments to the development of civil society. Bashiriyeh (ibid, p.1) states that civil society as a non-state sphere has been used in three senses within the western tradition:

> "First, as a condition obtaining before the formation of
> the state; secondly, as a condition opposed to the state

and thirdly as a condition emerging after the demise of
the state."

Civil society should be perceived in the modern era, and in Liberia in
particular, as a critical point of interaction and interpenetration of the
state system and countervailing social structures. This understanding
suggests a dialectic unity in which there is balance, but at the same time
constant struggles between the state and civil society structures. This
state of balance and mutual struggle also presupposes a metaphor for
continuous dialogue, critical reflection, challenge, conflict resolution,
renewal and qualitative growth.

Keane (1988,p.14) has defined civil society essentially from the point of
view of non-state activity:

> Civil society can be conceived as an aggregate of
> institutions whose members are engaged primarily in a
> complex of non-state activities- economic and cultural
> production, household life and voluntary associations-
> and who in this way preserve and transform their
> identity by exercising all sorts of pressures or controls
> on state institutions."

In their study, Jean Cohen and Andrew Arato defined civil society
in terms of the sphere of interaction between the economy and the
state. This sphere of interaction is composed of institutions such as the
family, voluntary organizations in the sphere of associational life, social
movements and "forms of public communication" (cited in Fleming,
2002,p.3). The Italian political economist Gramsci was a pioneer in
launching the process of elaborating three crucial components to the
understanding of civil society (Murphy, 2001). The first emphasis was
on the cultural and symbolic dimension of civil society. This dimension
determines the formation of action-orienting norms, values, meanings
and identifications.

The second dimension focused on the more creative side of civil society.
This includes social movements, collective political struggles, voluntary
associations, interest groups, informal networks etc., (see Flaming, 2002).
The third arena of civil society, to which modern social theorists have
made a key contribution to illuminating, involves the communicative,

deliberative conception of the public sphere. The public sphere is located in civil society and is where people can discuss issues of mutual concerns on the basis of equality. In a functioning democracy, the public sphere is a source of public opinion required to legitimate authority relations (Rutherfold, 2000). This understanding I believe is very important within the framework of the development of communicative competence in Liberia.

For, the success of the public sphere and civil society is determined by the pervasiveness of rational and critical discourse, predicated upon communicative competence and the power of argument. The success of the public sphere is also defined by self-governing decisions and choices of viable social and political forces operating within the realms of civil society. Michael Welton (1989, p.155) has referred to the initiation of social and political learning processes by critical adult educators and agents of change. Within these critical and collective learning processes one can identity the politics of influence, of inclusion, and the politics of reform and social transformation.

The process of dialogue, which takes place in the public sphere, is a learning process and can lead to the development of individual autonomy and self-determination. It is this process of learning that will eventually lead to self-emancipation within a collectivist framework in Liberia. Hence, one of the dangers of the overbearing state (leviathan), which we have seen time and again throughout the history of Liberia, has been the violation of the capacity of individuals and groups to formulate, rethink and recreate their lives in the space provided by civil society. But there is no doubt that only this process of renewal and constant rediscovery of national imperatives through public discourse can lead to the strengthening of civil society and the reorganization of the existing social order.

For, only self-emancipation and collective empowerment within the spheres of civil society, will deliver us from our national sins and set an ethical and corporatist agenda for a serious engagement with the most fundamental problems of national development. It also ultimately requires the reactivation of the spirit of voluntarism, which has always existed in the social sector as a veritable platform for social and political engagement.

Patterns of civil organization and critical consciousness

Empirical research conducted by Seibel and Massing in the 1970s argued that indigenous formal and informal organizations had long existed in Liberia. It was suggested that some of these organizations were often of ancient origin. These voluntary organizations were said to be dynamic and often adjusted to social and economic change thereby playing a major role in the transformation of traditional modes of production (Seibel and Massing, 1974). These patterns of civil and voluntary organizations that have long existed could be further nourished to enhance an incipient mode of critical consciousness in the social sector.

The outbreak of war and its subsequent aftermath saw the beginnings of new patterns of civil governance in Liberia, predicated upon the desire to form alternative and countervailing structures outside the narrow enclave of the state. What this suggests broadly speaking, is that there was a proliferation of largely self-governing structures, which form the social or non-governmental sector. These organizations, which are often referred to as NGOs, consist of a broad range of entities operating across a much wider spectrum of national endeavors. In 1991 the Interim Government of National Unity announced that there were not less than twenty international NGOs operating in the country. By now new organizations have cropped up while others have ceased their operations.

A typical example of organizations which have operated in the country includes Action Internationale Contre La Faim, Medicines Sans Frontiers of France, Catholic Relief Services, Christain Reformed World Relief Committee, Church World Service, Community of Caring, Plan International, World Vision, Adventist Development Relief Association, Baptist Relief, Oxfam, Save the Children Fund, the Christain Health Association of Liberia, Liberia Committee for Relief, Catholic Justice and Peace Commission, Special Emergency Life Food. Other organizations currently in existence include the International Foundation for

Education and Self-Help, the National Adult Education Association of Liberia, the Liberia Bible Translation and Literacy Organization, the Center for Democratic Empowerment (CEDE), National Human Rights Center of Liberia, Foundation for International Dignity, Association of Environmental Lawyers of Liberia, Liberia Democracy Watch etc.

These organizations have been concerned with local issues across all sectors ranging from the economy, human rights, public health, education, resettlement etc. These are the organizations that must constitute, through their public advocacies for constitutional rights and sound public policies, the locus of legitimate dialogic voices in civil society. These organizations must also constitute the focal point of learning and perspective transformation. The involvement of international NGOs is demonstrative of the fact that Liberia will need tremendous international support in accomplishing legitimate aspirations for social change.

In an era of globalization, the interdependency of nations calls for a collaborative spirit in tackling the challenges of underdevelopment and democratic change. International support and local endeavors in the social sector should be geared towards the fostering of critical consciousness and self-determination in civil society. The collective dimension of critical consciousness and perspective transformation cannot be underemphasized. An appreciation of the collective dimension of learning and transformative processes is critical to establishing the influence and legitimacy of the non-state sectors and their role in fostering social change in society.

In Paulo Freire's conceptualization of critical consciousness, education for self-emancipation is considered as a collective educational and learning activity, which has as its primary goal the object of social and political transformation. The most significant aspect of critical consciousness is the construct of power awareness. Power awareness is knowing that society can be remade by human action and by organized groups in society. This notion of power awareness is not only optimistic, but it is what must drive the social sector and lend it that sense of civic purpose and meaning, without which associational life is devoid of political and critical content. And this recognition should determine the educational and learning experience that lead to the attainment of critical consciousness and self-determination.

In the current situation of economic and political hopelessness, one must extol and call for the accentuation of the most progressive tendencies in an incipient social order in Liberian society. What distinguishes this incipient social order is seriousness in civic purpose and concerted efforts to harness a growing culture of self-reliance by the voluntary and non-state sector. This growing culture of self-governance at local levels is mainly embodied in the work of NGOs and those individuals who are determined to become autonomous agents of change. In these self-help organizations one can see the modest beginnings of a learning society and the foundations of a culture of collective social action. Through these NGOs, for example, Liberian youth have gained material support and emotional courage to build their knowledge and marketable skills, such as carpentry, tailoring, and entrepreneurial skills. Non-profit and non-governmental organizations (both local and international) also run adult literacy projects and vocational schools in Monrovia and various parts of the country.

Micro-enterprise training for private sector development and support programs run by NGOs often provide seed money and tool kits for trainees upon graduation, so that new skills can be put to immediate use for the benefits of individuals, their families and the larger society. Most of the financial support for these efforts have come from international and intergovernmental organizations such as the United Nations Development Program (UNDP), United Nations Scientific and Cultural Organization (UNESCO), and the United States Agency for International Development (USAID) etc. For example, UNDP has allocated US$1.3 million to support rehabilitation of the education sector to improve capacity in planning, supervising, monitoring, and evaluating.

These international organizations' support must be welcome. But they should readjust their policies by targeting resources to those areas that really matter in terms of the value they add to building a society that will not revert to the old ways of doing things. In the past, multilateral and bilateral financial support played a decisive role in prolonging the life span of dictatorial regimes in Liberia and in other non-democratic states, such as the Congo under President Maputo. This was done by often misdirecting development assistance, and without adequate emphasis on the building of accountability structures and indigenous social empowerment to ensure the proper allocation of donor assistance. Therefore, it is imperative that these international efforts—as helpful as they could be—— be complimented by internal mobilization of self-governing structures working to empower individuals and groups in civil society. There must also be an emphasis on developing partnerships and critical dialogue between the state, private sector, and civil society organizations.

Culture, symbols and self-determination

The cultural and symbolic dimension of civil society as determining the parameters for action-orienting norms and value systems have been emphasized by Gramci (Murphy, 2001) as indicated earlier. Thus, cultural and national symbols play a decisive role in organizing people for social action. Cultural values and symbolic representations of national identity are also often crystallized in the most cardinal principles, which undergird national policies. Such intellectual artifact and symbolic representation of national consciousness and aspirations is the national constitution. The constitution in any given society constitutes the basic and underlying framework document that embodies both the cultural and legal basis for promulgating national policies.

The Liberian constitution is no exception in this regard. Thus, chapter II article 5b of the current Liberian constitution leaves much to be desired in terms of our conceptual understanding of the cultural framework for national existence and socio-economic development. Chapter II article 5b of the Liberian constitution states (see Liberian constitution, http://www.repulicofliberia.com, p.4):

> "The republic shall preserve, protect and promote positive Liberian culture, ensuring that traditional values which are compatible with public policy and national progress are adopted and developed as an integral part of the growing needs of the Liberian society."

It is very difficult to determine what precisely is meant by the terms—"positive Liberian culture which are compatible with public policy." Is this positive Liberian culture organic enough to be representative of the virtues eminent in all indigenous cultural heritages? I mean cultural heritages that have evolved and adapted to the manifold social and historical processes in the sub-region? If this is the case, then no mention of such understanding is made in the current constitution. Constitutional language is important as it informs our political and institutional practices at the foundational level. There is no doubt that the use of language in such a symbolic document, whose provisions constitute first principles in organizing the basis for national life, has important ramifications in terms of power and dominance relationships in society. This understanding has been the preoccupation of speech act theory and contemporary socio-linguistics (see Bach and Harnish, 1992; Bach, 1987, 1994; Atlas, 1989).

It was Foucault who initiated the exploration of discourse by defining discourse as "the general domain of all statements, recognizing that these utterances had meanings and effects in the real world" (see Mills as cited in Paskett, 2001). Fairclough (ibid) developed the thesis that modern governments are particularly concerned with linkages between discourse, ideology and power relations within society. There are three different levels of discourse analysis in Fairclough's model (ibid).

The first level involves description at the level of the text to reveal its experiential, relational and expressive values. The second level involves interpretation and the third level involves explanation. Applying Fairclough's third level of discourse analysis to the interpretation of the text in article 5b of the Liberian constitution reveals that the text of this constitutional provision seeks to reinforce historical power relationships and a cultural paradigm undergirded by elite Anglo-American values. However, such socio-cultural assumptions do not occur in a vacuum in the Liberian context, as attested to by both the commonwealth constitution (adopted during the process of territorial consolidation) and the Greenleaf inspired constitution of 1847.

The commonwealth constitution of 1839 for example, made no mention of, nor indeed, showed any sensitivity to the cultural sensibilities of the indigenous inhabitants, who would be co-opted to constitute the future Liberian society and national polity. The Simon Greenleaf constitution of 1847, which would be only abrogated in 1980, can be portrayed in similar light. In these constitutional frameworks, there was no account of the compelling historical urgency to form an all-inclusive African identity, that valued all the good things embodied in the African heritage that persisted in the sub-region before the 1820s and after. In this particular context, one might add that Liberia was to ignore the warnings of Edward Blyden at its peril.

This section has sought to discuss the role of education in strengthening civil society in Liberia. The section has primarily sought to describe a concept of education as learning, which takes place in the process of critical discourse and interaction in the social sector. I believe that the concept of education as providing the tools to enable a more meaningful and productive engagement with the social and historical process must receive critical attention in the transformation process. This new educational challenge of fostering participatory discourse and social action, suggests that one must place premium on the critical role of cultural and power awareness, as the basis for attaining critical consciousness in civil society. Attempts to restructure the discourse of culture and power in the 1980s, and perhaps in the new millennium, have been dominated by two major approaches according to Giroux (1989, p.126):

> "In the first instance , there has been focus on the issues
> of everyday life and the insistence that cultures must
> be analyzed in their particular, concrete, historical, and
> social forms. The emphasis here has been on forms of
> consciousness, experience, and the subjective side of
> human relations. Power in this case has been linked
> to culture through the ways in which particular social
> and class formations are either constrained or enabled
> to produce their own experiences and histories
> around emancipatory goals...In the second instance,
> the emphasis shifts to the notion of subjectivities
> are produced and therefore must be analyzed as the
> effect of wider social forms. Meaning is derived in this

approach less in the consciousness of social actions than in the forms of language, narrative, and other sign systems that position subjects within specific webs of possibility."

In view of the discussion in this section, two interrelated judgments can be rendered: 1) The process of national renewal requires strengthening civil society through the formation of countervailing social structures, to enhance the functional capabilities of the state; 2) The process of nation building must be rooted in a sense of a new cultural and national identity. This conclusion is particularly important for Liberia as the country is expected to head towards general elections in 2005.

II
International dimensions of educational programming in postwar Liberia

Liberia is today a country in dire need of international assistance as the result of years of political chaos and economic mismanagement. The Liberian economy was already in deep crisis prior to the Taylor led invasion in December 1989. For example, during the 1980s, the gross national product (GNP) decreased by 2 to 3 percent annually. The 1988 education expenditures amounted to only 17.5 percent of total government spending. This number has since reduced considerably owing to uninterrupted disruptions to economic activities and lifelines. The Taylor regime could not even provide electricity to Monrovia, the capital, within seven years of its rule let alone provide the needed resources to boast educational development.

The country lies today at an important historical crossroad as the many challenges facing her are enormous, to say the least. Indeed, the gravity of the humanitarian challenges facing this oldest of African countries, in the wake of recent fighting is simply awesome in its depths and unmitigated proportions. Entire towns and cities have been laid to waste and the country has been transformed into a huge wasteland. There was widespread uncertainty among the general populace at the dawn of the inauguration of the post Taylor interim administration of warlords and politicians.

The basic infrastructure for long-term recovery and institutional landscapes are bleak in the face of a total breakdown of order and indigenous support frameworks and systems. But when the dust settles and calm is returned to the nation, the nature of the educational and human resource development policies will to a large extent determine the success or failure of comprehensive disarmament and demobilization—the most important challenge in this initial phase of the postwar period. Thus, the success or failure of comprehensive disarmament and reintegration of former combatants will determine the success or failure of the transition process, which has been underway in Liberia since last October, 2003.

Consequently, it is not far fetch to assume that formal education and short term training programs will be required to underpin disarmament, counseling and the provision of adequate short-term opportunities to replace the temptations for continuous warfare. At the critical intersection of educational policy and political dispositions, disarmament and demobilization must be viewed as a process rather then a series of staged events (see Johnson, 2004). Thus, the disarmament of school age boys and girls and young adults and their eventual re-integration into society will hinge upon the availability of schools, training facilities and the provision of appropriate curriculum resources to support learning. The education sector in Liberia should be reactivated to meet this vital and basic need of a society, which must recover from long years of neglect. The achievement of this enterprise would call for massive United States and multilateral support and fundamental reforms at the basic level.

For example, classroom methods should be reappraised to foster a permeable, co-constructionist and intra-cultural curriculum perspective that fits our aspirations in a postwar period and for the 21st century. This new approach and curriculum framework would take due account of learning and cognitive styles and differentiations in the milieu of cultural socialization (see Johnson, 2001). In Liberia in all these years before and after my days as a school boy in Firestone, the gains brought about elsewhere by applying the lessons of the modern cognitive revolution and experientialism have never really filtered through to positively affect classroom learning and instructional practices.

Thus, to improve the quality of instruction and learning in Liberia, there must be a paradigm shift within the context of a new curriculum theory and institutional processes. There should also be emphasis on the proper training of teachers, counselors and social workers to improve efficiency and optimization of output. Similarly, funding priorities and principles of strategic planning would have to be reassessed to augment a new policy orientation of change and forward movement. An adjunct to these foundational reforms would be an alignment in current United States assistance with indigenous strategic goals and principles.

Order of priorities to foster peace and educational development

There are many priorities and challenges that lie ahead as the country slowly moves into a postwar period. The first order of priorities for the new interim administration in the transition process, however, would be to begin a credible process of disarmament and eventual dismantling of all armed groups in the country. This step would contribute tremendously to reinforce the impulses and current moves toward sustainable peace. It would also without much doubt help to aid the expansion of a refocused and restructured education sector, as it includes former combatants; a great number of whom have repeatedly expressed their desire to go back to school or join some training program.

The system must be reactivated to include them (after proper screening) in a variety of learning and counseling formats, to ensure complete rehabilitation and readiness for productive life in the mainstream of society. In fact we may have already seen major steps through deliberate acts of courage to began this process in earnest as we have heard reports of former combatants voluntarily surrendering their weapons to United Nations (UNMIL) peacekeepers. Up to press time it has been reported by UNMIL that more than 30,000 ex-combatants have already been disarm. This is absolutely good news!

However, revitalizing the education sector in Liberia will in no small measure depend on American support and policies toward educational development in Liberia. The United States and Liberia are bounded together by historical ties and a strategic partnership in the past, which spanned many years. Most Liberians would agree that the United States must take the lead in galvanizing support for funding and promoting quantitative and qualitative growth of the education sector. Structural and contextual changes in curricula formats and processes, the strengthening of accountability systems in schools and financial support for capital constructions of new schools and colleges around the country, would be required to meet the challenges of ensuring competent civil governance and sustainable peace in the future.

These are the historical imperatives of a new era that must be met through productive partnerships with the United States and other important donors in the international community. Hence, there should be United States and international support earmarked for development in various time frames including short, medium and long terms. But these arrangements would have to take place against the background of certain foundational perspectives and assumptions, regarding the not so categorical distinctions between what is and what ought to be, in anticipating a new orientation in educational policy and practice that sustains peace and distributive justice.

The process of revamping national policies and the educational mission in Liberia must be predicated upon solid foundations and a host of considered theoretical perspectives. In the past this was never the case, and thus planning and strategic vision gave way to guess work and an essentially haphazard approach. These observations are not new, they were made in the past in numerous World Bank education sector reports in the late 1970s by various panel of experts who worked in Liberia. In departing from a failed past, one should seek to acknowledge that there are several important foundational principles, which must guide the transition toward stability and change in the education and social sector. I would wish to outline some of these key foundational perspectives and underlying operational assumptions. It is suggested that these assumptions and operational premises should undergird new perspectives in charting a responsible course toward democratic self-governance, and in the formulation of public policy and strategic commitments.

Foundational perspectives and working assumptions

An integral component of these perspectives and working assumptions is the premise that sound educational foundations are an integral part of nation building, especially in a country that would have to start from building new foundations due to widespread destruction. Another premise is the acknowledgement that education must serve both as institutional and psychological frameworks for empowering citizens to become autonomous and rational decision makers in pursuing alternative paths toward personal and collective transformations. One should accept the fact that this operational path is indispensable to growth in the education sector and a transformed institutional setting for civil governance, despite the current status quo of chaos and far from responsible leadership.

A third foundational understanding places premium on a solid manpower, community, and human resource development policy orientation. This understanding provides a critical link to success in building a viable and productive postwar civil and constitutional community. The last and equally important assumption is that United States and donor support for the education sector can be made more meaningful by transcending its current approach. The modus operandi for critical success must be expansive and developmental in its basic orientation. Current and past approaches by the United States and UNESCO for example, have lacked a developmental and strategic perspective because they have primarily focused on short-term gains. American support for education over the years primarily in the form of USAID short-term development grants has induced indirect and haphazard assistance, thereby imposing undue limitations on desirable outcomes. What is needed in Liberia today in postwar conditions is a collaborative approach based on common understanding and adequate needs assessment, program implementation and evaluation. This collaborative approach must also be duly underpinned by the appropriate institutional and development analysis.

Hence, for there to be a radical change in resource allocation strategies and an enabling of the process of national reconstruction, this support in whatever form must not be coincidental, but rather firmly tied and integrated into a workable and comprehensive countrywide policy framework for human resource and manpower development. This integrated approach is the critical link that has been missing in our conceptual understanding and practice of educational development in the past. But such a link must now be created in the fostering of self-determined and self-governing individuals and structures to ensure sustainable peace.

Thus, it is through the operationalization of the above foundational assumptions and other unstipulated but essential variables that would decidedly lead to recovery, as the nation is about to set on a new course of peace and sustainable development in securing a future. These working assumptions, which should serve as guideposts for future policy interventions, must be further elaborated upon against a critical understanding of the limits of previous structures of intervention, to restructure education and improve its technical efficiency by the principal donors in the international community.

Educational funding and distributive justice

In the theory of justice, the most common criteria of distributive justice are equity, equality and need (see Maiese, 2004). Economic resources and educational goods and benefits are often distributed among various members of society on the basis of the above criteria. It is a matter of historical fact that how the decision has been made to distribute economic goods and benefits in society have always determined the nature of the economic system and a society's social formation. For example, the philosopher John Rawls have claimed that the role of distributed justice is to restrict the influence of luck in the distribution of benefits so that these goods might be distributed more fairly and to everyone's advantage (ibid, p.2). A logical outcome of this opinion in the realm of public policy might be to put more emphasis on education so that the long-term influence of luck might become minimized.

Educational funding, which also depends on a philosophy of distribution of economic benefits, is central to the formation of a new methodological perspective in the construction of a more functional learning society.

This view has been amplified in the changing paradigms of educational reforms in terms of global educational agendas over the years. For example, in World Bank circles, various levels of education have been earmarked for support and active assistance at different times in congruent with the results of marginal economic returns to education analyses.

Thus during the 1980s, a wave of education sector reforms based on cost recovery in secondary education was admonished by the World Bank in various sub-Saharan African countries that had pledged to undertake structural reforms and adjustment of their economies. These reforms which continued up to present in some cases, constituted part and parcel of the package of measures and adjustment conditionality that borrowing countries had to fulfill to get loans and other financial support to finance development across the board.

There are mixed results in terms of the overall success of structural adjustment at the macroeconomic and sectoral levels in sub-Saharan Africa and in other borrowing countries. And it is also not certain if adjustment policies have had any positive effect in eliminating income disparities (see Hinchliff, 1989; Fuller, 1989; Hutchful, 1994). Reimers (1994) has employed a hypothetical counterfactual methodology, which covered 8 years of the adjustment period in a controlled group of countries. His counterfactual analysis showed that contributions of households to education declined dramatically in adjusting countries compared to non-adjusting countries.

In the mist of these structural reforms in Tanzania, for example, public spending on education fell to just over 4 percent in the early 1980s compared to the pre-adjustment period, and then dropped to below 4 percent by the early 1990s. Public spending to improve education actually declined in real terms over time in conditions of engineered fiscal retrenchment. Around 14 sub-Saharan African countries have cut per capital spending on education under adjustment programs proposed by the World Bank and International Monetary Fund (IMF). Countries such as Niger, Zimbabwe and Zambia have cut spending on education by 3 percent per annum under adjustment regimes.

What these examples show is that educational development in postwar Liberia will not be necessarily about policy choices to support a particular level of education or about merely introducing and sustaining cost recovery and user charges to supplement government support. It is clear that introducing user charges across the board as a way of raising funds to finance needed structural changes will not suffice given that gainful employment and other income generating activities have collapsed. Cost recovery as a fiscal tool to improve the quality of educational inputs would have to be extremely selective in current economic and social circumstances.

For the economic and fiscal outlook in Liberia in the short term is bleak as has been attested to in the submission of Jacques Klein to the Security Council of the United Nations. Indeed, the Liberian economy is in dire straits as the result of massive looting and destruction occasioned by recent fighting and long years of neglect. Employment generation in the private sector will not be forthcoming until the sector has regained some semblance of general health. Unemployment and underemployment in the economy hovered around 80 percent during the tenure of the previous administration.

Thus, the number of people living in poverty has progressed geometrically particularly under the criminal regime of Charles Taylor. Today more than 80 percent of the population lives below the poverty line. Because of the lack of policy direction, discipline and fiscal prudence under Taylor, the economy had not only been stagnant, but it was bedeviled by crippling structural and institutional rigidities, such as chronic and widespread corruption and lack of policies for structural diversification. At the end of the 1990s, the Debt-Service-to-Exports ratio in Liberia was 70.8 percent. What this suggests is that the country was paying more than 70 percent of her export earnings to service debts owed to various categories of borrowers.

The current outlook may even be worst given the total breakdown in economic activity. Under current fiscal arrangements it is clear that the country would be incapable of meeting pressing economic and social challenges. Hence, structural adjustment in the social sector will be needed, but this must however be conducted on different terms that might doubtless conflict with prevailing orthodoxies and assumptions. In order to ensure distributive justice and equal treatment as a primary objective of the new educational agenda, and across-the-board-support for all levels of education, readjustment would be simply untenable without the requisite concerns about the distributive aspects of economic growth. This is why one would be very careful of conducting reforms within the spirit of the principles and neo-liberal dispositions of the Bretton Woods Institutions (World Bank and IMF) without regards to the historical concerns of economic and social justice.

Thus, the central challenge going forward is to adopt a strategic vision to optimize output in the short and long runs. In effect this calls for an activist and balanced developmental perspective. And this is where United States support will be needed to help design a strategic and an overarching framework for human resource and institutional development in postwar Liberia. There must be financial and material support from the United States and other donors to ensure the implementation of a comprehensive development plan for each region and segment of the population to ensure a much fairer distribution of scarce resources. This is the basis for the workable partnership I would allude to.

The current fixation on humanitarian and relief assistance, which fits the mood of the times given the immediate humanitarian crisis, may not be sufficient for sustainable long-term recovery as we gradually move into a phase of relative stability at the end of conflict. The United States support could be critical in assisting to cancel Liberia's national debt or at the minimum helping to put a freeze on debt servicing for a specified period of time. Another area where United States support would be invaluable could be the recovering of looted assets amassed by Charles Taylor and his criminal gangs and hidden away in a web of secret Swiss Bank accounts (see Johnson, 2004).

These times of hardships in Liberia will require United States support and assistance more than ever before. The depths of the development crisis in Liberia as the result of long years of civil conflict and neglect will demand a new American attitude of total involvement and compassion for a country, which is in many ways a product of American history and civilization. Such total approach in order to succeed must be radically different from United States attitude to Liberia in the past. Since its origins as a supposed save haven for ex-slaves from the United States in the 19th century, successive American administrations have always shown a noncommittal attitude to matters concerning Liberia and its well-being. This attitude dates back in earnest in the 1820s and perhaps earlier when the idea of Liberia was being considered.

In 1906 the Liberian Government under President Arthur Barclay, after realizing that it was impossible to borrow money from local German merchants, negotiated for a $500,000 British loan, through Sir Harry Johnston, a British colonial agent, and his Liberian Development Company. But Sir Harry Johnston would later admit in his book "The Story of Life" that the loan was not a legitimate business transaction, but rather it was used as a trap to limit Liberia's independence and subject it to the "colonial claws" of the British Empire. There are other examples in which previous Liberian leaders chose to enter into inequitable and dubious diplomatic and financial arrangements with European Powers and private business interests, because of the absence of sustained United States support and involvement in Liberia.

But this must change not only for Liberia's sake but also for sustaining America's strategic interest and influence in the region. The United States should not only come when they need something from us, but they must come when we need something that would be of mutual benefit to both parties. And there is no doubt that actively supporting the growth of institutions and social forces for self-governance and self-reliance will be in the long-term geo-political and strategic interest of the United States in the sub-region. Through self-reliance, civil society in Liberia will gain the confidence in its moral and political commitment to democratic virtues and to become a seat for meaningful critical discourses for the advancement of the public good.

Building upon existing foundations

The new strategic approach to educational development must be built on a logical symmetry between a host of programs and intentions. This follows that educational programming in Liberia must built upon new foundations that would seek to harness American support for the social and nongovernmental sectors through deliberate and coordinated policy action. Today, the social and nongovernmental organizations have become enablers in civil society through their proactive engagement in the most diverse national endeavors ranging from trading, health care, human rights issues, conflict resolution, education and training. The new educational agenda must seek to empower these self-governing structures by strengthening accountability, training and professional expertise. This new agenda in tandem with the general theme of this book must be undergirded by judicious and systematic recourse to the framing of popular consensus through dialogue.

The relative success of the social and nongovernmental sectors has reinforced the notion that the process of ensuring a fair and equitable distribution of social and educational benefits must start with efforts to empower decision makers at the local level. This would ensure more powers to democratically elected provincial leaders and autonomy among villages, towns, counties and households to effect real time decisions that cater to their interests on the ground. In essence, the object of this new vision would be to break the bonds of the patronage system, which has done so much damage in the past. Part of this strategic vision to refocus decision-making is for the United States and donor partners to contribute to an information technology and communications fund. Liberians of reputable standing must also be strongly encouraged to contribute toward this fund.

This fund could be used to expand broadcasting and telecommunications networks throughout the country and to provide the infrastructure and platform for the creation of a 21st century distance learning and extension education program in farming communities and other relevant geographic localities. There may also be the need for the formation of an axis of symmetry between various policy actors as emphasized earlier. Creating synergy between local and external approaches to educational programming would help to reduce waste, duplication of efforts and generally assist the rational allocations of scarce resources to meet desirable political and social outcomes consistent with the aspirations of a new era.

This section has reflected the challenges facing Liberia at a very defining moment and crucial juncture in its Liberia. Thus, it is suggested that the country will need a fundamental reappraisal of the educational mission to formulate policies that would be consistent with current demands. Consequently, I have sought to highlight the need to foster a new educational agenda that would be anchored on a strategic vision and productive partnerships. This vision must be predicated upon the formation of a viable partnership with the United States that would lead to the preservation of the enlightened mutual interests of both countries. This follows that the country will need financial and material resources, which would be forthcoming through the United States and the support of other principal donors such as the United Nations and other non-governmental organizations (NGOs).

This new policy vision in Liberia must also lead to the decentralization of decision making to introduce built-in flexibility and accountability in the system, which would in turn undermine the deleterious effects of patronage as a culturally and institutionally entrenched endogenous variable. Similarly, I have also concluded that the country would need structural realignment between various policy approaches to stop wastage and duplication of efforts at all levels of the education system in Liberia. As I have emphasized throughout this book, at the foundation of this realignment will be continuous dialogue and the seeking of practical consensus in the way ahead. Ultimately, this is the platform that must be established for laying a solid foundation for sound governance and economic vibrancy in the postwar era.

Chapter summary

This chapter has demonstrated how education and learning are important to the building of a viable civil society and democratic culture. I have posited in this chapter that the relationship between civil society and the state must be based on trust, collaboration and dialogic understanding. It must also be based on productive partnerships with the international community in a time of need. I have looked at how a sense of solidarity, cultural values and share historical destiny are important concomitants of a vibrant civil society. I have drawn readers attention to a variety of views regarding the potential of discourse as an instrument of self-determination in civil society.

I looked at Gramcian perspectives in terms of how civil society is actually the sphere of interaction of diverse social-historical forces operating outside the purview of the state. This is very important, given the longstanding problems of the overbearing tendencies embedded in state structures and other presidential prerogatives in Liberia. This speaks to the question of how to limit the exploitative and colonizing tendencies of the state through communicative action and emancipatory education. The creative side of civil society such as voluntary associations, NGOs, and other interest groups must be rediscovered within the construction of a broader narrative that embraces social action and democratic self-governance.

Chapter 5

Discourse on war and conflict resolution

"In such a dialogical situation one also needs to learn to understand, respect and accept the reasonableness of the other. This means that one starts to accept the possibility of pluralism. This experience of pluralism as legitimate needs to be integrated through reflection, both personally and in a group."

—Amaladoss, 2004—

I need not repeat in this section what I have already emphasized in previous chapters. For, everybody would readily agree that Liberia is at an important historical crossroad at this particular moment. This succinct realization suggests that we have two stark choices that confront us. We must either consolidate current gains on the path of national reconstruction through the assistance of the international community, or choose to fall into the abyss of darkness. These choices demand active and unrelenting discussions and appropriate policy interventions to propel us into a post-conflict and more humane phase of social and political development.

At the heart of conflict resolution, as the epigraph to this chapter suggests; lies honest, reasonable and participatory discourse about the requisite strategies to adopt in mapping a future without constant recourse to political violence as a first option in resolving the most profound issues of governance and distributive justice. This chapter is divided into four main sections. The sections in the chapter will examine the causes of the breakdown of constitutional order such as the absence of participatory democracy and the distortion of authority relations. I will seek to make some suggestions regarding how to restore hope and stability to our body politic and social system through transformation and by reconstituting interlocking social and power relations.

I
National conflict and social change in Liberia

Paternalism and the overbearing nature of the state have been cited as a principled reason for conflict and the collapse of the Liberian state. This overbearing state has overtime stifled the growth of a democratic culture and economic forces. But what is needed in the country to tackle this issue is undoubtedly an overarching process of social change. Amos Sawyer (2004,p.2) reinforces this notion in a letter to the current Chairman of the National Transitional Government of Liberia:

> "Beyond the issues of reform specified in the mandate
> of the Government Reform Commission laid out in the
> Comprehensive Peace Agreement, Liberia faces deep-
> rooted challenges that cannot be swept under the rug.
> Our country has been in the throes of violent conflicts
> for about a quarter of a century. Before then, the storms
> had been gathering for decades. Our political system
> seems entrapped in a cyclical pattern of zero-sum

politics- violent breakdowns- acrimonious elections-
zero-sum politics."

Democratic social change in Liberia requires the presence of particular
forms of construal and solidarity. This solidarity must foster collective
consciousness and the recognition that in terms of tackling issues of
national affairs, one is always engaged in a process larger than the
individual and his or her idiosyncratic interests. This realization is critical
to social transformation and the dawning of a new era in Liberia.

The mystique of presidential power in Liberia is closely linked to the lack
of functioning institutions and the distortion of the role and influence of
existing ones, such as the courts, traditional societies, public associations
and other pillars of civil society. The pathology of personal and individual
power in Liberia must be replaced by the ideals of institutional power
and the fostering of communicative competence at all levels of the social
system. An ideology of institutional power is ultimately undergirded by
mass participation of all the people in how they are being governed.
It requires new principles of resource distribution in Liberia where
significant stakeholders will have a say in making those vital decisions
that affect their lives on a regular basis. When these principles have not
been instituted, we have seen nothing but contempt for the views of
persons, lower level decision-makers and entire regions. The former
superintendent of Lofa County, E. Sumo Jones (2004,p. 5) captures a
classic example in his recent article on constitutional change in Liberia:

> "As if awarding the construction contract to someone
> from without the county with no reference to us with
> funds not owned by the Government was not enough,
> the Government again ordered the County to give the
> remaining $43,000.00 to the Lutheran Church to assist it
> in erecting a girl's hostel on the campus of the Lutheran
> Training Institute (LTI) which was already under
> construction. Before we could give the amount to the
> Church, its representative declined to accept the grant
> with the excuse that they already budgeted adequate
> funds to build the hostel. The central Government in the
> fact of the Church's refusal to accept the $43,000.00 and

the County not being, at least, consulted to be deprived its badly needed funds, we were, again, ordered to let a local authority of the Church have the $43,000.00 to be deposited into his account until such time that the Church stood in need of the amount. We, again complied with that order and have yet to know what ever was done with that money that the County's people sacrificed to pay for a particular development purpose which amount we did not intend to be deprived of without our prior consent."

How such a system based on rational discourse and our good intuitive instincts and impulses to do what is right for the betterment of all can be created is the monumental challenge facing the Liberian nation. The fostering of communicative competence through dialogue in public institutions means that people would have equal opportunity to participate in public discourse, as such that what they think and say would have the requisite moral and political authority, subject to consensual validation and logical criticism. This is the new society to which I have inspired, struggled, and for which I have devoted the last four years trying to conceptualize in some of its complex and multiple dimensions.

Principally, this is the great challenge because of which I have been inspired to write this book. It is a challenge that have somewhat been met to reasonable degrees by what I would refer to as the great nations. In the experiences of the great nations, such as some of the more developed societies, institutional power has always been legitimated by dialogic and democratic voices including all sections of society. The critical observer would note that the structure of national failure and persistent conflict in Liberia could be principally located within the vortex of the pathology of personal power, and the psychosocial assumptions and web of psychic delusions, which substantiate and give it its lifeblood. What this presupposes is that the analysis of political and structural failure should be predicated upon bringing into conscious awareness the role of subjective and phenomenological factors. This is another important dimension, which resonates in this book. Focusing on subjectivity in social analysis is a delicate process that focuses on the individual as a unit of analysis. This approach reinforces the assumption that personal transformation is inextricably linked to social transformation. It is worth quoting Dorothy Ettling (2003, p.13) who has elaborated on this position:

> "In our studies, we found a voiced connection between personal empowerment and concern for the larger issues of social change within the women with whom we worked. They were eager to contribute their experience and ideas towards solutions on larger issues of poverty and domestic violence. They consistently stated not only their desire to contribute to the discussion but sought means to take action within their immediate circles or in the larger public arena."

The merits of the subjectivist approach, for example, primarily lie in the analytical achievement of Fanon's subjectivist methodology and other phenomenological perspectives in the theory of motivation. By shifting the analysis of colonialism away from economic and political factors, Fanon succeeded where many structuralist theorists of decolonization had essentially failed. He plumbed the deeps of subjectivity in the construction of the colonizer and colonized as racialized subjects, thereby aptly specifying the differential paths of the neuroses generated by colonial domination and the imperial enterprise in subject territories (see Fanon, 1952;1967). Similarly, the decomposition of Soviet Power in Eastern and Central Europe in 1980s and 1990s, has amply demonstrated the limits of the predictive power of structural determinism as a framework for emancipatory praxis and social change.

The Charles Taylor factor and individualism

A phenomenological approach would lead to elucidating the underlying motivations of a character like Charles Taylor and his tiny band of marauders and political sycophants. This approach would lead to the generation of interesting research questions. For example, it would lead to such questions as: What are the subjective and objective factors that propelled or motivate the likes of Charles Taylor into action? What really made him to do what he did as a political actor? Could his actions and choices be traced to dramatic events in his childhood or pre-adult life? What methods does he use to evaluate the consequences and justifications of his actions and beliefs? Does his actions signify the rise of a more destructive variety of individualism[22] in Liberian society? Was he merely a product of a cultural and institutional system as I have tried to postulate in this book? How would one justify that his actions were motivated by rational self-interest or a rational competitive impulse? These would be very interesting questions to pose and probe among many other possible questions and hypotheses (see ibid).

Indeed, the social psychologist would be interested in knowing, ultimately, why a single individual or a tiny group of individuals would inflict so much havoc on millions of their compatriots through their actions and choices, just as Hitler did in the 1930s and 1940s.[23] While some of the old class of established politicians in the country and political activists of the 1970s and 1980s sought to appease and aid the Taylor assault on the Liberian people, others were completely unable to provide any vision or concrete political program for civil and emancipatory action. Partly because of the failure of the established class of political leaders, individuals of good moral standing and character have been sidelined in the corridors of political power for almost a generation and perhaps more. And there is little doubt that this may be one of the prime reasons for national failure and decline in Liberian society, which must now be addressed.

[22] Lange et al (1997, p.733) have proposed a three-category typology of social value orientation, examining differences between pro-social, individualistic, and competitive orientations. The authors suggest "these orientations are partially rooted in different patterns of social interaction as experienced during the periods spanning early childhood to young adulthood." Social value orientations are shaped by social interaction during early adulthood, middle adulthood and old age.

[23] On December 29, 1989, the country was plunged into a civil war that has lasted for the last 14 years. The National Patriotic Front rebels who invaded the country in 1989 were under the command of a former Director General of the General Services Agency in Liberia, Mr. Charles Taylor. As most African despots and rebel leaders, Mr. Taylor claimed to have come to liberate the people from dictatorship and the misrule of the late Army Sergeant Mr. Samuel K. Doe.

In a new era of social change and public accountability, public service should become more attractive by providing a moral incentive for people of honorable character to contribute their quota toward progress; it should not become an institution that legitimates the greed and twisted aspirations of those with dubious distinctions. This overriding objective can only be achieved through pragmatic leadership, corporatism and a sustained process of institution building to deepen national reconstruction efforts. This suggests once again that we must heed the lessons of the most successful nation states, without by any means ignoring the particularities of our historical development.

In the war of African independence in the 1950s and 1960s, modernization scholars of the West including Rostow, Parsons, Eisenstadt and others argued that the functional diffusion of capital in Africa would lead to social change and economic progress, and build institutional capacities that would eventually minimize the propensity for political violence and civil strife. In Taylor's world and political calculations, this paradigm was completely turned on its head. He had sought systematically and strategically to spread violence throughout the region without a constructive program regarding how to evolve social systems that would ensure political sustainability and cope with the dynamics of modernity in our times. Of course one needs not be reminded that part of the problem that brought us here was the deliberate and immediate recourse to violence by self-styled liberators, after the ill-fated and much compromised elections of August 1997.

I would argue that the August 1997 elections were compromised because they were not merely the outcome of the wishes of the Liberian people, but rather they were the result of political expediency and a war fatigue syndrome, which had afflicted the major players and principals in West Africa after almost ten years of conflict and mutual destruction in Liberia. Many Liberians and pro democracy and human rights activists believe this. It is worth quoting aspects of an interview of Conmany Wesseh- a prominent Liberian politician and pro democracy activist, conducted in 1998 by Glenn Baker of America's Defense Monitor:

Glen Baker: So again, you were telling me about efforts at— after the election, about the impact of weapons on the election process there.

Conmany Wesseh: Well, basically what I've been saying is that there has been a negative impact of weapons, light weapons, on the peace building process in Liberia. In the first instance, it was because of light weapons that so many people got killed and so much destruction, and the disease and hunger that are the defect of fear. Running in the displacement into refugees camp, over half of the – about half of the population in the refugee camps…Then into the election process, which is supposed to help to settle the leadership question, we've found that light arms – the fear of that, of light arms—led to an election which was free, but wasn't fair. It was free because people didn't have arms hanging around the place. On the day of the election, there were no such arms. But those who voted knew that the arms were right in the corner, and therefore, they voted for the one who they perceived had the biggest arms, and the lightest number of arms. Now, that affected the results of the elections.

Political expediency in the West African region and beyond is one of the external dimensions of failure, which must not go uncheck. This was why the success of the peace process in Ghana was very important and had to be approached with the lessons of the numerous rounds of negotiations prior to August 1997 in mind. I hope this time no warring faction would be allowed to determine how Liberians will live a generation from now. This is the ultimate test of the courage and character of the current generation of civil society and political leaders. Thus, the great historic challenge is to not repeat the mistakes of the past, by allowing the followers of Charles Taylor and other rebel factions to manipulate the process at the disadvantage of the popular will and aspirations for democracy and stability.

The demands of justice and national reconciliation

Given the nature of the Liberian conflict, it would be difficult to achieve lasting peace and national reconciliation without moral and legal accountability for wanton acts of violence and crimes committed against the innocents. All attempts to set up a war crimes tribunal in Liberia were fiercely resisted by the sitting administration and its apologists for very obvious reasons. But Liberians and the international community must now insist that there should be appropriate legal and punitive sanctions against those found guilty of committing crimes against humanity during the past and in the current conflict. This is a more durable means of ensuring that wanton acts of violence against the innocent for any purposes will not be repeated. Conflicts and acts of institutional violence in society have a dynamic nature. Thus, conflict resolution methods must try to come to terms with the changing nature of conflict and violence in society. Using the South African situation as a case example, Simpson (2004, p.2) has succinctly commented to this effect:

> "In the re-building of such fractured societies, attempts at reconstruction and reconciliation have to come to terms with the changing nature of conflict and violence, rather than focusing on a simple end to such conflict. Amidst all the dramatic change taking place, certain sustained features of marginalization, impoverishment, and relative deprivation remain at the root of ongoing criminal violence in South Africa in the post-apartheid era- in much the same manner as they underpinned political violence and conflict during apartheid. The extent to which this violence transmutes itself, belying any notion of a clear or rigid dividing line between political, criminal and social violence, presents a primary challenge to sustainable reconstruction and reconciliation in societies emerging from autocratic rule or from intense civil warfare."

Given this understanding as cited above, it may be impossible to achieve lasting peace in Liberia without proper accountability for wrongdoings during the last 14 years. Proper accountability structures to avenge wrongdoings in one form or the other may help to purge our culture of an emerging pattern and practice of violence. The indictment against Charles Taylor for the greatest responsibility for crimes against humanity in Sierra Leone by the Special Tribunal is a very good start on a long path towards atonement. While one may regard the lack of proper institutional means to execute the indictment at the time it was issued as being problematic, the integrity of the Special Tribunal on this particular issue is beyond reproach.

Similarly, the evocation of political sovereignty to question the justifications of the court's action is injudicious and merely peripheral, it doesn't speak to the core issues and the most burning questions at stake. Some commentators have even spoken of embarrassments to sovereign governments, the demands of African traditions etc., to question the legitimacy and timing of the court's actions. The most burning questions in Liberia today concerns how to curb the reasons for anarchy and national failure in our community, and Charles Taylor happens to be one of those decisive reasons. Like all other great questions of national survival and historical continuity, this question is a strategic one that demands a critically reflective approach. In this process it must also gain priority over other tactical considerations. Thus, removing Mr. Taylor from office given the changed political and military realities, which had obtained on the ground was as important as beginning the long process of institution building in Liberia to arrest the causes of perennial civil crises and national failures.

Thus, within the parameters of reason, civility and decency, the cause of saving lives and humanity is always higher than claims to notional sovereignty. This was the cause during the ECOWAS intervention in the early 1990s, and it is also the case with the United Nations approved special court in Sierra Leone. For what is the value of the sovereignty of political authority as may be expressed in presidential immunity, if such authority has been so perverted that it becomes an epicenter of a system of violence destroying the lives of peoples in countless communities? Liberia must move forward! One must read the signs and seek to delimit the field of psychological influence of presidential authority in Liberia, for it has caused so much damage in cognitive, material, human and cultural terms.

Perhaps delimiting the influence and mystification of presidential authority in Liberia, which is now a historical imperative, is not only a critical challenge for institution builders, but it is also the task of agents of cultural change. There should be the realization that in any historical community, political authority must never be allowed to exist in a vacuum, it is the people who giveth legitimacy to that authority and it is they who taketh it away! There is a priori justification based on the psychological need for security (see Maslow, 1954) to assume that people in the sub-region would like to see their suffering come to an end.

On the other hand, one is yet to view any empirical evidence, which suggests that it would not have been in the best interest of the Liberian people and the people of the entire sub-region to indict Charles Taylor for crimes against humanity. One is yet to see proof that the timing of the indictment was inappropriate when everyone knew that Mr. Taylor's positions regarding the current peace process changed with the minutes. At one moment he was saying this and at another moment he was saying something else. Conversely, the indictment had only served to change the political dynamic by enabling the agents of change, while sending a very potent signal to would be gangsters and liberators, who had aspired to take Charles Taylor place through the most undemocratic means.

Moving toward a polycentric social order

In Liberia there is only one future devoid of frequent violent ruptures, and that is a future in a polycentric social order. Autocracy and the untold damages caused by personal power have made it abundantly clear that multiple centers of decision-making that affect the most varied aspects of our lives is the only logical path to prosperity and sustainable peace. Local leaders and citizens as well as stakeholders must be empowered to become masters of their own destinies and active participants in the remaking of their social and economic conditions. For some who are very used to the old ways of doing things, this process may require a fundamental transformation in their meaning perspectives and schemes.

Because change in Liberia is not only a matter of praxis, but it is also a process of coming to terms with our prior interpretations, predispositions, norms and criteria of examining the validity of our claims and actions. The changes required involve experiencing a deep, structural shift in terms of the basic premises of our thought, feelings, and actions. These changes also involve what I would refer to as a major historical undertaking to understand ourselves and self-locations and our relationships with other human beings and with other external realities.

They involve our understanding of relations of power in interlocking structures of class, gender etc. Ultimately, change in Liberia has to do with digging dip into our souls and reexamining the very core of our existential realities and social consciousness at various levels of the body politic. A polycentric social order in Liberia will involve strengthening civil society and guaranteeing individual rights through the formation of countervailing social structures to enhance the functional capabilities of the state. The necessary and sufficient conditions for achieving these lofty and practical ideals consist of the willingness to accept and become a part of a change process. This is the ultimate test that determines success or failures in the grand scheme of things. This is the gateway to ending the Liberian tragedy and to constructing the basis for political sustainability, economic, social and institutional growth.

II
Pragmatics and miscommunication in political discourse

When past leaders have not kept their promises and stuck to their "grand visions" of society that they themselves enunciated, instances of civic courage have been few and far between. A leader can only inspire by leading by example and showing the courage to stick to ethical and moral principles. This is an important hallmark of a theory of discourse democracy within the public spheres; when leaders and politicians are held accountable for what they say and what they promise that they would do. This is also truly the hallmark of ideal speech situations and unfettered communication within a given society and culture.

Thus, the proliferation of ideal speech situations or power free communication must be a desirable goal in Liberia in the face of systemic breakdown of organizational and institutional processes. It is the pursuit of these ideals that have inspired my thoughts in this section. The section discusses paradigm cases of the effects of miscommunication in Liberian political discourse. The central hypothesis, which has formed the governing principle of my analysis, is that the Austinian construct of illocutionary speech act is as important in everyday communication as it is in the realm of rational discourse. I have concluded by arguing that the truth of assertions in the context of constructive social action truly lies in the realm of pragmatics.

Austinian pragmatics

In the history of language and modern philosophy, *pragmatics,* has become a separate field of linguistics and the philosophy of language, exercising the minds of philosophers and linguists alike, since Austin's 1955 Harvard lectures (first published in 1962) in which he laid the groundwork for what would become speech act theory. Austin's theoretical preoccupation in these lectures was to construct dialogue systems that would give accounts of aspects of meaning in which coherent sequences of verbal interactions would become apparent.

In Austin's conceptual model, utterances or speaking is viewed as a kind of action being performed by the speaker. To speak or make an utterance in this sense is primarily to perform an action. What this suggests is that the basic sentence type in language is declarative (i.e. a statement or assertion). If a speaker utters a sentence such as: [I promise to take a taxi home], what the speaker is actually doing is making a promise rather than just describing one. Austin described this kind of utterance as performative utterances. In making performative utterances, the speaker performs the action named by the first verb in the sentence. We could insert any number of adverbs, such as *hereby* etc. to stress the performative functions in the execution of meaning.

The emphasis in Austin's speech act theory is not on the truthfulness or falsity of assertions, but it is rather on whether these assertions work or not. Thus, for assertions or utterances to work, they must meet certain felicity conditions. These felicity or enabling conditions for a performative include social conventions, procedural and ceremonial features governing speech acts etc. Without satisfying these felicity conditions, it is possible to conclude that a speech act does not work. For example, if the current government of Liberia declares that the country is a functioning constitutional democracy, without any intent to follow the constitution and other conventions, which ensure the realization of such assertions, then such peformative could be deemed infelicitous because it does not work. Such a speech act would be described as a misfire in Austin's terminology. Austin went on to add sincerity clauses to his felicity conditions, such that if one insincerely performs a speech act by [making a promise] when one clearly intends to break such promise, such an act would be described as an abuse of a speech act. Making a promise also falls within the category of commisives. This class is characterized by committing the speaker to do something by making a promise.

The possibility that a speech act could be abused leads us to making a crucial taxonomic distinction between three different types of speech acts. Hence, Austin distinguishes between locutionary act, illocutionary act and perlocutionary act. However, the theoretical preoccupation of Searl (a prolific contributor to speech act literature) is not so much to focus on the divisions between categories of speech acts as described by Austin. Searl (1969:17) on commenting on the significance of speech act theory had this to say:

> "[A] theory of language is part of a theory of action, simply because speaking is a rule-governed form of behavior. Now, being rule-governed, it has formal features, which admit of independent study. But a study purely of those formal features, without a study of their role in speech acts, would be like a formal study of the currency and credit systems of economies without a study of the role of currency and credit in economic transactions. A great deal can be said in the study of language without studying speech acts, because any such purely formal theory is necessarily incomplete. It would be as if baseball were studied only as a formal system of rules and not as a game."

The focus of Searl's work has been to refine Austin's work on speech acts by providing the necessary and sufficient conditions for the demonstration of different types of illocutionary acts (see Bach, 2003). An illocutionary act is the action intended by the speaker when he/she makes an utterance. Austin and his successors including Searl, have been mainly concerned with the uses to which language can be put in society. This is why the term speech acts is often used with the meaning of illocutionary acts in mind. What the distinction between illocution and locution signals perhaps is a clear division of labor between semantics and pragmatics. The demarcation suggests that *semantics* focuses on the meaning of utterances as viewed out of context, while *pragmatics* focuses on the performative and situational force of utterances. And this in my view transcends an ordinary analysis of sentence structures to construct meaning. It also applies to linguistic units in the check for pragmatic implications of specific utterances. Thus, like Austin, Searl and others who have come after them, I am also concerned with the effects of illocutionary acts. One of my central objectives in this section, therefore, is to review paradigm cases of illocutionary acts and their material effects on politics and popular discourse in Liberian society.

The effects of miscommunication in political discourse

There are two main strategic considerations in assessing the content of what Searl (1969; see also Bach and Harnish, 1979) considers the illocutionary point of a speech act. These considerations include the psychological state of the speaker (state of mind), or what one might refer to in Mezirow's terms albeit with some qualifications, as habits of mind. Habits of mind are frames of reference and ways in which one interprets the world predicated upon specific psychosocial and pyschocultural assumptions. In assessing the content and illocutionary point of a specific speech act, what one is primarily concerned about is the fit between an assertion and the world. For example, if a speaker issues a directive or makes a request or orders someone else to do something, what he/she is trying to do is to change the world so that it matches his/ her utterance. Thus, the question of fittingness between words and deeds, which is also a question about the relationship between thinking and reality, falls within the dual realms of psychology and philosophy. It encompasses various domains of philosophy such as epistemology, ontology, logic and perhaps metaphysics. This question may also belong to the domain of cognitive psychology.

I will now turn to how illocutionary speech acts have played out in the evolution of political discourse in the Liberian society. My objective, which has been laid out earlier, is to review paradigm cases and their effects on structuring interaction and political dialogues in Liberian society. Examples of paradigm cases that immediately come to mind in this context are the numerous speeches by various Liberian Presidents and Civic and Community leaders in times of great uncertainties or to commemorate national occasions, or just merely to make policy pronouncements to the Liberian public. Dissecting these speeches and political commentaries has both a heuristic and practical value. It enables us to evaluate the distance between words and reality. It is ultimately indispensable to gaining a critical understanding of how particular historical figures have affected the nature of popular discourse and its impact on the evolution of the social system.

Importantly, and, as I have stated elsewhere (see Johnson, 2002), there is a need to elaborate explanatory models that illuminate the biographical and idiosyncratic circumstances of significant actors in the movement of history such as leaders. So, one is attempting to do just that by critically assessing the utterances of public figures and influential opinion makers in society. One of the objectives of such assessment is also to uncover epistemic errors, delusions and self-deceptions, which may derive from the effects of miscommunication in public discourse.

Thus, political battle cries issued by past and present political leaders to arouse public sentiments and action also falls in the category of paradigm cases. In addition, other instances that also spring to mind are declaratives in the form of views and assertions found in the current body of literature that constitutes Liberian Studies. Of course I am not referring here to everyday speech acts per se, however, I would contend that there is a vast similarity between such speech acts and what Searl refers to as the *propositional content* of political discourse and communication.

For example, the intent to deceive or persuade others to execute specific actions (public or public) is as much a feature of everyday speech acts as it a characteristic of public and academic discourse. Thus, bringing private and public discourses into the domain of a rational thought process lies at the heart of Habermas's communicative action. Communicative action in such context adds a dimension of rationality to the necessary and sufficient conditions expounded by Searl or indeed, the all-important sincerity clauses outlined by Austin. Habermas has specified communicative action as (cited in Szczelkun, 1999, p. 1):

> "The concept of communicative action presupposes the use of language as a medium for a kind of reaching understanding, in the course of which participants, through relating to a world, reciprocally raise validity claims that can be accepted or contested."

In his inaugural address upon his ascension to the presidency in 1944, William V.S. Tubman had this rather strong and resounding message to convey to his listeners (Wreh, 1976, pp35-36; see also Gaunnu, 1980):

> "Fear no man, honor and respect lawful and constituted authority, yield a cheerful obedience to and live within the law. Mark you well I do not advocate license, nor will any such attitude be tolerated. But I advocate fearlessness and stamina in our people acquiring and possessing property, in exercising and pursuing peace, prosperity and security...We shall endeavor, therefore, to stimulate and encourage the development of courageous and fearless manhood, to look to this great cause and to the preservation in full force of our democratic superstructure, and by wise and constitutional measures seek to promote intelligence among the people as the best means of preserving our liberties- to see to it that Liberty and Law march hand in hand."

In this inaugural address, Tubman makes reference to the importance of preserving in "full force our democratic superstructure," but in the course of time his actions came to resemble something else. The reality and context of Tubman's politics was to undermine the very foundations of this democratic superstructure he alludes to by suppressing any avenue for public criticism of his policies and actions. There are so many instances throughout the administration of Tubman, which attests to this. They include for example, the various false assassination plots to eliminate perceived enemies, corruption, the maintenance of a blotted bureaucracy, the excesses of the open-door policy as a development strategy, the willful suppression of student activists and political opponents etc.

There is a great disparity between the above assertions about the preservation of a democratic superstructure in Liberia in the turbulent aftermath of World War II and the subsequent propensity to pursue policy actions in contradistinction to these declared principles. Examining the performative force of Tubman's utterance in 1944 suggests that the utterance fails to fulfill the sincerity conditions of an illocutionary act. There is a clear contradiction between a promise made on this occasion and the intensions or the will to carry it out.

The assertion could therefore be described as a misfire or the abuse of a speech act. I have no illusions, however, that the tension that often exists between intensions, statements and subsequent actions constitute a difficult philosophical conundrum. Perhaps the difficulty in this terrain primarily derives from the inherently fallible and imperfect nature of our understanding of the world in which we live. For this reason there are no absolute truths, and therefore, one could only speak of contingent validation of social ideas and norms of appropriateness. As the saying goes, what is science and appropriate today may soon be considered non-science and inappropriate tomorrow. This revelation has been one of the enduring contributions of Karl Popper to the development of philosophical thought (see Soros, 1998). George Soros (ibid, p.ix) has stated that:

> "I was influenced by Karl Popper, the philosopher of science, whose book *Open Society and its Enemies* made sense of the Nazi and Communist regimes that I had experienced first hand as an adolescent in Hungary. Those regimes had a common feature: They laid claim to the ultimate truth and they imposed their views on the world by the use of force. Popper proposed a different form of social organization, one that recognized that nobody has access to the ultimate truth. Our understanding of the world in which we live is inherently imperfect and a perfect society is unattainable."

When a group of leaders of political parties and other interest groups came together recently in the United States and declared that they are the primary stakeholders in the political process in Liberia, either they lack the proper information to make the correct judgment that the people through their elected representatives are the genuine stakeholders in the political process, or that they intent to impose their will on the Liberian people. Either way, it is difficult to make a judgment when an action has not yet been taken. To make a rational and reflective judgment in this case demands a concrete analysis of psychological states, intentions, wills etc. Such reflective exercise in rational judgment constitutes the true spirit of communicative action, which involves the reciprocal validation of knowledge claims. But the only thing one could modestly declare at this stage is that the assertion by the political parties amounts to a miscommunication of perhaps their intensions, strategies and policies in the pragmatic realm.

In his critique of "Liberian Political Science" Patrick Burrows (1989) offers a definition of the term oligarchy that seems to challenge the empirical validation of the notion that an "Americo-Liberian oligarchy" existed in Liberia prior to the April 12th 1980 coup. Thus, Burrow asserts on page 32 of his monograph in reference to Fahnbulleh's remarks:

> "Fahnbulleh often refers to the "Americo-Liberian aristocracy" or "oligarchy" implying hereditary privilege or corruption involving a few families. However, the evidence presented in his book does not support the notion that privilege was transmitted within selected families from one generation to another. The author has yet to show that the descendents of Hilary Teage and Joseph Jenkins Roberts, for example, held privilege positions during the Tubman era...Our analyst would be hard-pressed to show that local presidents came to office by means more corrupt than those employed elsewhere."

In our search for consensual, contingent and reciprocal validation of ideas through rational discourse and critical reflection, which is a hall mark of a true scientific and speech community, it is possible to agree with Fahnbulleh, Liebenow, and others who have argued that an

Americo-Liberian oligarchy did indeed, exist in Liberia at least prior to the April 12th 1980 coup. Importantly, the weight of evidence seems be in their favor when one simply examines the dictionary definition of the word oligarchy. The definition of the word oligarchy as provided by the Columbia Encyclopedia (2001), indicates that the term oligarchy is a Greek word-meaning rule by the few.

This Columbia Encyclopedia also shows that the classical definition of the term given by Aristotle is the same; a government by a few, usually the rich, for their own advantage. The fact that Tubman or Tolbert may not have been related to Joseph Jenkins Roberts and Hilary Teage by blood doesn't really matter in this case. There was at least a 100 years reign by an Americo-Liberian oligarchy in Liberia, largely through the institutional instrumentality of the True Whig Party and other non-democratic civil structures. Now, this reign was in contrast to democracy, which is usually a system in which elites compete with each other, gaining power through "unimpeded" popular suffrage. Basil Davidson (1992:247) has embodied these sentiments in his writings (see Chapter one).

Far from "eurocentric privileging" and "essentialism" as Burrows claims, what this analysis shows is that there is a gap between Burrow's assertions on this particular score and the reality of Liberian politics for more than a century. The gap between speech and reality in this case like in other paradigm cases discussed earlier, questions the truthfulness of his assertions from a pragmatic viewpoint.

President Tolbert came to power in the aftermath of Tubman's death and made this solemn pledge to uphold the salient principles, which guarantee the rights of all in his first inaugural address on January 3,1972 (see Gaunnu, 1980:399):

> "All this I see, and yet still further beyond the horizon, bursting upon my sights, I behold the beauty of a Glorious Land of Liberty, wherein the dignity of mankind takes the clearest precedence over the selfishness of men; where respect for inalienable and fundamental rights and imperishable principles are placed wholly above impelling expediency, in the exercise of power

and privilege… I perceive a nation reaching toward the wider perspectives of ingrained morality, upon which the larger judgment of history will depend. Unfolding the scroll of a fuller destiny, I see our people enjoying the blessings of unbounded fulfillment, by the grace of Almighty God."

These lines described part of the vision of Tolbert as laid out in his first inaugural address to the Liberian nation. There is no doubt that the idealistic principles embedded in this speech should be worthy of any nation, especially one that was originally set up to be a save haven for suffering humanity. However, the critical analyst would discern a big gap between this rhetoric and historical reality. Firstly, President Tolbert failed on the economic front due to internal and external pressures. Secondly, and more significantly, he tried to liberalize the political system to accommodate dissent but was unwilling to go as far as was being demanded by an increasingly radicalized opposition, clamoring for a faster pace in social and political reforms.

The Tolbert administration was a missed opportunity by all stakeholders in Liberian society, because it led to the rise of destructive militarism and brute force as a weapon in the political field. Liberia and its people are reeling from this missed opportunity right at this moment. In the post Tolbert era, naked brutality and mindless violence have become a credo in the mode of functioning and social practices of men and women who would ignore rational discourse as a torchlight in the path ahead. It seems the breakdown of the Tolbert regime foreclosed all opportunities for gradual reforms in the political and social realms. The opportunity for dialogue and rational public discourse had been sealed and it would remain so for an entire generation. As the saying goes, when our people are not under the palaver hut trying to settle disputes amicably and charting the future, they may be engaged in infriticidal warfare— killing one another. Thus, rational discourse within the public domain is an authentic and logically alternative path to greater wisdom, freedom, peace and self–determination.

This section has reviewed perhaps a very minute portion of the many effects of miscommunication in Liberian politics over the years. The central hypothesis, which has formed the governing principle of my analysis, is that the Austinian construct of illocutionary act is as important in everyday speech acts as it is in the realm of rational discourse. In this particular connection, the section reviewed what I would refer to as paradigm cases of illocutionary speech acts in the evolution of discourse in Liberian politics and its analysis. I recognize the fact that the emphasis in Austin's speech act theory is not on the truthfulness or falsity of particular speech acts. However, I wish to conclude that in the context of constructive social action, the truth of assertions truly lies in the realm of pragmatics. What the field of pragmatics does in terms of the underlying objectives of this book is to reinforce the role of rational discourse and reflective judgment as being critical to the project of constituting new organizing principles and institutional patterns and frameworks for conflict resolution in Liberia.

III
A Symposium

The premise and basic rationale of this section is that both the necessary and sufficient conditions for rational discourse have rarely existed in the field of social policy in Liberia. This has been primarily so because of the distorting influences of tradition and political autocracy. But now the country is situated at a major historical crossroad when it has become imperative to dialogue, reflect and take action to empower social forces to instigate a radical break with the past through institutional and political change. I would argue that such process of critical reflection, dialogue, and action is akin to a process of social learning as have been reflected throughout this book. Mezirow (1991,p.190) has intimated that "critical reflection, discourse, and action can change culturally assimilated assumptions and premises which limit and distort understanding and give learners greater control over their lives." Just to re-emphasize what I have already indicated above, it is fair to argue that among the many reasons for state failure, as manifested in the failures of most Liberian leaders, is the lack of what Mezirow has come to refer to as systemic critical reflection of assumptions.

This type of reflection involves critical reflection on one's assumptions pertaining to the linguistic, political, economic and other taken-for-

140

granted cultural systems in society. Chris Argyris and Donald Schon (1978) have distinguished single-loop learning from double-loop learning in their exploration of organizations as learning systems. Single-loop learning seems to be present when values, frameworks, and strategies are taken for granted. But in double-loop learning, learning involves the modification of the underlying principles and policies of an organization or institutional system. There is symmetry between double-loop learning, which no less involves significant learning, and systemic critical reflection of assumptions. These paradigms of what I would call social learning are critical to our understanding of human action as a product of various forms of consciousness.

Ellen Sirleaf (1999) has reported that the Samuel Doe regime, like its predecessors, could not meet the popular expectations of the Liberian people by formulating a vision for a country long in need of institutional and political change. This was because the coup leaders were essentially a product of the value system and political culture of the past and were thus unwilling to free themselves from the pathologies and psychological trappings of that past. What took place, then, on April 12th 1980, was a passing of the guard from a tired and failed True Whig Party to a band of marauding soldiers who would systemically unlash havoc on all sections of society. Lacking coherent economic and social policies, the Doe regime sought to rule by fear and the brute use of force. It is no coincidence that the brutal and despotic policies of the Doe regime in the 1980s helped plunged Liberia into a 14-year civil war and constitutional collapse. Hence, to assert that the country must now recover from this state of collapse would be an understatement.

This section is an attempt at constructing an imaginary dialogue among past and present Liberian leaders. It is a hypothetical scenario intended to show how power free communications, where everyone has an equal opportunity to participate would look like in practice. The dialogue is based on the features of Plato's symposium and its central objective is to shed light on those factors that limit understanding, social cognition, and the ability to take positive action in the political and institutional realms (see Rachal, 2003). The most distinctive feature of Plato's symposium is that Socrates and his peers gather for a dinner and drinking party at the home of Agathon of Athens to discuss the category of love in all its complexities and variable dimensions (ibid). In this imagined symposium, past and present Liberian leaders, without the boundaries of time and space, have gathered to ponder over several critical paradoxes. These paradoxes regard the causes and consequences of political autocracy and the resulting betrayal of a nation.

The accounts presented in these exchanges are both fictional and a representation of original, primary and secondary sources. I believe that the origins of Liberia's troubles, like the history of all human conflicts, can be traced in its past. By trying to retrace this past, distant and immediate, I have attempted to add a new dimension to our critical discourses. In this pertinent and crucial context, this section is also an exercise in reflection and social criticism. It will also ultimately help to magnify my essential thesis that the way to peaceful coexistence in Liberia lies in the power of communicative action, which is already imbedded in our culture. I shall return to this point later in this chapter.

Samuel K. Doe [1980-1990]: We came to power on April 12,1980 to extinguish political autocracy. Our actions, preoccupations and underlying motivations were purely altruistic. I would submit here to you all that we did achieve a lot for the nine years we still in office. Why can't everyone see that? While didn't Charles Taylor and his followers see that? The fact that no one can see that to me is a principal paradox!

William Tolbert [1971-1980]: I am glad that we have congregated here today to take stock and ponder over some fundamental issues. What this thing about paradox? There is another important question I must pose immediately. Are we arguing here today that the search for paradox is a search for an explanation of state failure in Liberia? In what way does this constitute a general understanding? My good old friends, I maybe inclined to think that we might have already discovered a conceptual framework for our dialogue.

Amos Sawyer [1991-1994]: By paradox, do you mean that the views of the Liberian people are contrary to received wisdom on this matter? Or have they unfairly denigrated your achievements and "lofty" aspirations? Do you mean that you were hailed as liberators and healers, and yet, in the fullness of time you proved to be a curse and blight on the nation?

Thus, your term in office was tumultuous times indeed! Those times were extraordinary years as some of my good old friends have claimed in their writings!

Samuel K. Doe [1980-1990]: I would not put it quite like that? If you like we can examine the records. I am certain that we would soon realize that my assertions about our achievements in office are correct. In fact you would see that any contrary opinion simply amounts to a paradox, because that would be an opinion with infinitely contradictory qualities.

William Tolbert [1971-1980]: Let's examine the records; I believe that it is in my prime interest to do so. I also believe that it would be in the interest of posterity to dig out the facts. As you might know, it is also in the interest of the living to undertake such endeavor. I say this because I now believe in the notion of fallibility, meaning simply that we must always try to improve our understanding of the forces that drive our motivations and actions, both in the past and in the present. Being the president of our country in the 1970s, and for few months in 1980, has taught me one cardinal lesson. That lesson is that our search for meaning must always be a departure from errors, not merely a search for absolute truths. In fact I no longer believe in absolute truths. Indeed, the search for reasons to justify actions can never be a search for absolute truths. I make these utterances knowing fully well that I may be contradicting the gist of my own argument as the great thinkers have claimed (see Burbles, 1993).

Amos Sawyer [1991-1994]: I wish you had known that prior to your inauguration in 1971 Mr. Tolbert. I wish you had come to terms with the true meaning of that postulate, say, at least by 1973. Perhaps there would have been enough time to recover and restructure the civil discourses of our nation. I would suppose that if that had been the case, then, the outcome of our collective history would have been different. If that had been the case, perhaps Samuel K. Doe and his band of lumpen proletarians and marauders would not have seized power in 1980.

Samuel K. Doe [1980-1990]: Don't' you think that is too optimistic a view of Liberian history? In fact, was such a monumental change possible by merely restructuring discourse and political institutions within less than a decade? Is that what you are claiming here today my old friend?

Amos Sawyer [1991-1994]: Well, I am an eternal optimist if that is the case. I always believe in the powers of creative and positive agency. What I am simply saying is that change is always possible because humans, through their individual and collective actions, are always capable of fostering change. In other words, what seems to be permanent is the contingent and transient quality of the capacity to foster change in the human condition.

Samuel K. Doe [1980-1990]: Your assertions indicate that you may be a very cunning and slake intellectual. Because you are sophisticated at your trade, you may be adept at navigating the most difficult terrains by always walking the middle path. It seems as though you always maintain a sense of balance in your politics. Perhaps your statement here is a testament to that. You seem to have an infinite reservoir of hymns that you employ to suit all occasions! I have observed this in my numerous dealings with you especially when I enlisted your services to advise me on cultural policy and intertribal relations. I believe that is a more distinctive feature of your character, which I admire, but perhaps, others might view cynically.

Charles Taylor [1997-2003]: Let us now examine the record of my good old friend Samuel K. Doe as he has requested. I hope my coming into the fray, as a "revolutionary fighter" in 1989 would be thoroughly appreciated once this critical examination is done. For a starter, in 1986 the good old gentleman was kind enough to admit that the Liberian economy was on the verge of total collapse due to mismanagement. Around this period, the monetary economy declined by more than $100 million due largely to capital flight, and the cumulative budget deficits exceeded $900 million. The economic wrongdoings of this administration were catalogued in a number of reports such as the Jeffy Commission report of 1983, the economic memorandum prepared for the donors' conference of 1983 etc. (Sawyer, 1988). By 1989 economic growth had granted to complete halt as the situation worsened by the day on the monetary and fiscal fronts. The extraordinary years of the Doe regime were, indeed, distinguished by deepening economic recession and a subversion of constitutional principles, interpretation and order.

Amos Sawyer [1991-1994]: Did you use the monograph I wrote about the Samuel Doe regime in the 1980s as a source for your arguments? Your arguments here today sound exactly like every account I had in that monograph. As you may be aware, the accounts in that monograph were later amplified in a subsequent volume in which I sought to elaborate on the trajectory of our collective failings within the span of almost a century and a half. You may be aware that I was not only preoccupied with the failings of the Doe regime. In that work I sought to elaborate a conceptual framework that would explain the emergence of autocracy in Liberia among others. I know you have said all the right things about the excesses of the Doe regime, but I must hasten to inform you that I strongly detest your advocacies and brand of revolutionary change. Your model of a revolutionary transformation was a calamitous infamy in the history of all humanity! Your merciless purging of conscienscious objectors smacks of the days of the Chinese infamous "cultural revolution" and the "great leap forward" as a growth model in terms of its totalitarian dimensions. If I may add, this has turned you and your cheering supporters into some of the worst abusers of human rights ever to visit planet earth. I also find wanting your perspectives on economic change, regional stability and the nature of justice. In general, your philosophy of power baffles me and shall continue to do so to the end of my days. I have exercised my mind regarding what I could have done or not done to stop you during the heydays of your venomous crusade. I have imagined many scenarios in my mind's eye, but all I can say now is what if, what if!

Samuel K. Doe [1980-1990]: As a fully functioning adult, I have now come to the conclusion, albeit upon critical reflection and hard introspection, that ethnic nativism is the greatest evil in political and social life. If I had known, I would not have sought to construct an ethnic based political hegemony on the basis of an obnoxious paradigm. I would have striven for the development of an all inclusive and authentic national consciousness. I say this because I realize that there is more to unite than divide us as a people. We often say we are one but our practice creates the impression that that is not so. And this to me is a paradox, specifying a contradiction between speech and action. The second group of peoples, the Kumbas, who arrived in our region, came from the Western Sudan around 6,000 B.C. As you may be aware this was even before the beginning of the transatlantic slave trade.

The third group of peoples including the Bassa, Kru, Dei, Mamba etc. also came to this region as the result of population and political pressures in the Western Sudan. The last group of tribes to arrived here, such as the Mandingo and the Vai, also originated in the Western Sudan. Their migration toward what is now known as Liberia was prompted by the victory of Askia Mohammed, which reduced the Empire of Mali in the sixteen century. It is not my place and I have no intension of making an exegesis of historical texts. I leave the business of interpretation and criticism to the scholars. My message here is a simple one that says that the sooner we realize that we may all have the same origins the better. Oh! By the way! The first group of inhabitants that lived in Liberia were Pygmies, as has been recorded by the Liberian historian Abayomi Karnga (see Karnga, 1926).

William V.S. Tubman [1944-1971]: Your metamorphosis regarding matters of conscience and national integration is very impressive Mr. Doe. I wish I were around in the 1980s to show you the ropes. I am sure you may have heard from someone that I had an explicit national integration and unification policy. How times have change! However, I must admit that I was not impressed with your performance on the economic front. You inherited an economy that was in some trouble but you did little to halt the decline, instead, your judgments were so myopic that they actually led to further decline. During my administration, I opted for an explicit and strategic vision that would be undergirded by an exogenously induced economic growth. This meant that I was going to leave no stone unturned in encouraging inward investment in Liberia. Thus, the economy experienced extensive growth during my tenure. From 1946 to 1960, we attracted $500 million in foreign investment.

Exports rose from $15.8 million in 1948 to $82.6 million in 1960, an increase of 422.8 percent; and Government revenue rose from $32.4 million in 1960 to $69.9 million in 1971, an increase of 115.7 percent. I strongly believe that we did achieve a lot during long tenure, although my detractors like Robert Clower and his team of experts from that "bloody" Northwestern University in the United States have attempted to subvert the truth. Did they really appreciate the value of apprenticeship education in the legal professions with a provincial flavor? There have been talk of "growth without development" and widespread political repression in the immediate postwar years and subsequently. Everything I did during my administration I thought was in the interest of modernization of an essentially backward and pre-capitalist society. Ours was a "forced march" and a struggle for modernity, and of course hearts and minds. This is while I had little regrets for using the stake ever so often, even if they interfered and impeded the normal democratic and institutional growth of the nation. I did exactly what my communist nemesis, Joseph Stalin, would have done to turn around old, tired and Czarist Russia.

Charles Gyude Bryant [2003-Present]: I want to see this country move forward and be at ease with itself as it was in the past. But I have no illusions that this can only happen without retribution. Retribution is a circular notion in terms of pure justice. The pleads for justice is sound but it must be based on the principle of forgiveness. "Let by-gones be by-gones as they say in the Liberian vernacular." Forgiveness is the underpinning logic of the politics of empowerment, diversity and inclusiveness. I would argue that there is an element of collective quit in all of us because everyone did something wrong to somebody during the war. However, I would not say that I am sure anybody beside me shares this judgment. Well, maybe a few of my friends and cheering supporters!

Joseph J. Roberts [1847-1856; 1872-1876]: I do not envy your position Mr. Bryant. But you will have to rethink your principle of justice. I am saddened to note that things had to turn out this way after almost 200 years. It is sad that our country had to go through all these troubles for the last 25 years. Most of the problems that are confronting you today originated in the beginnings of our great patrimony. There were both conceptual and practical difficulties associated with the enterprise of building a "Christian Civilization" on the West Coast of Africa. There were issues of identity and representation in the constitution of order, which we did not do well in tackling. I now have serous doubts that declaring independence (statehood) on July 27,1847 was the right thing to do. It may have been too early, coming in less than 28 years after the first settlement was formed on the Atlantic Coast. This is just one of several alternative hypothesis. For, I am not unaware that this presupposition may be challenged by several counterarguments, such as the claims on Liberian territory by the French and the British leading up to 1847. Hence, the declaration of independence at the time it did may be rationalized by the imperial and unsavory territorial ambitions of the French and the British in our sub-region in the 19th century.

But I will go back to the point that we were not ready, and perhaps, this is while most of the colonists opposed the idea. There was a cycle of dependence on the American Colonization Society (ACS), embedded in the paternalism of an earlier antebellum period. This dependence was a double-edged sword. While it was necessary to some degree especially in the initial phase, it later became a psychological and institutional burden that had to be eradicated. As Wilmont Blyden, a former President of Liberia College, observed in the 19th century, most of the people who lived in settler society at that time refused to economically and culturally divorce themselves from the United States.

This attachment was subsequently embodied in most cultural and national symbols such as the flag, the constitution and the names of towns and cities. I would argue that it was this attachment that would impinge upon our relations with our tribal brethrens and thus forming a contributive factor for state failure. It led to a convoluted system of settler nativism that would come to haunt us in the long run. And, as the economist John Maynard Keynes says, in the long run we are all dead! What is saddened to note here today is that we the leaders did nothing to discourage this drift. Now, could you argue that this was a deliberate act of national betrayal on the part of people who were mere armatures in the craft of state building? About that I am not too sure!

David Kpomakpor [1994-1995]: But Mr. Roberts the fact that you were mere armatures in state building does not explain away the grievous errors that you may have conducted. You may be underestimating the nature and significance of free choice and wills in your presentation. For me to except your argument on this account, therefore, you would have to convince me that free choice did not play a part as a determinative variable in your political calculus. And may I submit that that would be a very tall order given the empirical evidence, which exists to the contrary. Your eminence, let me inform you that I have read with great interest the 1825,1839 and 1847 constitutions, and what I see presents a different picture from your representations of reality on this particular matter.

Edward J. Roye [1870-1871]: It was not only the conservatism of the Republican Party prior to 1870 that held us back as a nation. Roberts has made reference to the drift and lack of purpose regarding matters of integration and the development of a national consciousness. I understand that the True Whig Party also had an unenviable record. Although, I recon that the history of settler society and of our country in general is incomplete without the story of the racial skirmishes that unfolded in earlier times. It is important to know how this story impacted on future political developments and our national character. One of my most pernicious follies was my attempt to subvert the electoral process partly in response to the politics of character assassination.[4] This attempted unconstitutional action on our part led to my arbitrary dismissal by my political foes, which in turn helped to sow the seeds of autocracy in Liberia. You may argue that this is a stretch. But this is by no means a remote affair looking back almost two centuries ago, but one must see in our actions the beginnings of the formation of political autocracy. These were decisive and defining moments in the history of our commonwealth when the constitution and democratic protocol gave way to mob action and chaos. "What one has sowed one shall reap!" If you know what I mean!

Joseph J. Roberts [1847-1856; 1872-1876]: I am not sure how this process can be about apportioning blame. I regard our historic exchanges here as an exercise in self-examination and reflective criticism. This being the case, I should draw your attention to a cardinal aspect of the language question in our national development. During the enlightenment, the Europeans from Kant to Hume to Willem Bosman etc. fabricated various myths and made presuppositions regarding our race and the connection between literacy and intelligence, albeit a tenuous connection sometimes. There is an individual that goes by the name of Dualu Bukele. This contemporary of ours single-handedly created a writing system for the Vai language. We did not take notice because we had no regard for the vitality of "native culture."

By creating a syllabary, which was so popularly accepted among the Vai that by the end of the 19th century most of them were using it, this man was doing something probably as great as some of the finest achievements of an era of reason. I wish we had had a language policy that took notice during the course of settlement activities in the 1820s and thereafter. It was very important that an African culture could produce its own system of writing in an age where writing was viewed as the most visible sign of reason and by extension, human intelligence.[5] Dualu Bukele achieved that, but up to this point the significance of his achievement outside the walls of the University of Liberia has never been truly acknowledged.

Arthur Barclay [1904-1912]: I wish I had implemented the United States President William Howard Taft commission's recommendations in 1908. The commission's report made it clear that European colonialism was less of a threat to our sovereignty then the chaotic state of our economy and public administration.

William Tolbert [1971-1980]: Both of you gentlemen are right about every point you have just made. One of my other regrets in office was the fact that I did not succeed in renegotiating all the terms of the Firestone concession agreement especially in terms of the construction of the tire plant issue. I would choose not to go into the history of how and while Firestone came to Liberia in the 1920s. One thing I know is that we were sold short by the Firestone agreement. There were many provisions, that if we had our way, we would wish to erase. It is the type of agreement that any future democratic government must avoid if Liberia is to develop. The new economic foundations must be based on mutual reciprocity, indigenous capacity building for industrialization, and self-sufficiency. Anyway, such were the times, the politics and the conditions! The paradox that exists with regards to Firestone is that this was supposed to be the path to economic takeoff, but in actuality it turned out to be a trap for neo-colonial exploitation, and what the Neo-Marxist Samin Amin calls "maldevelopment." No one would have known in the 1920s what Firestone would amount to for our people. It is interesting to note how some of our African American cousins across the Atlantic were very enthusiastic about the Firestone contract. In 1925 a writer in the Chicago defender praised Harvey Firestone as "a great man with a great wisdom" whose plantations would benefit not only Liberians but also African Americans. In the same year another newspaper elaborated on the significance of the Firestone agreement (see Sundiata, 1990,p.65):

> "At the Census of 1920 only one colored man in the entire country gave his occupation as that of a forester; fifty reported themselves as architects; eighty as civil engineers and thirty-one as mechanical engineers... due to the fact so few of our young men have taken up these professions, because of the difficulty of obtaining employment. It appears that the Firestone Company may be obliged to select a mixed, if not all-white administrative force to put over this great piece of constructive work in the black Republic, in whose progress all of us are greatly interested."

Samuel K. Doe [1980-1990]: Like President Tubman, I am also a free trader. Your statement amounts to an indictment of free trade and the very logic of liberal economics. At least that is the way I see it. There are contradictions inherent in an agreement like that where the profit motive is not far from the corner, as one would expect. But are you saying that we should then conclude that liberal economics or free trade is a paradox because of the costs of capitalist investments? Maybe the real paradox lies in the dichotomy between our speech and actions. The relative costs and benefits of capitalist expansion don't always suggest a fate accompli in terms of losers and gainers. In other words, this may be more about what we do in terms of the management of our interests than what we say we intend to do. Thus, the battleground must be expanded and reshaped to include the field of interpretive discourse and positive action.

Joseph J. Roberts [1847-1856; 1872-1876]: I guess we are all capitalists in the pantheon of economic policies, maxims and institutional ideals. Yes, free traders we are! There is the messianic purpose and there is the profit motive. It was the quest for business ventures and profit that served as the pull and push factors for some of us to the Atlantic Coast. But what we failed to realize was that our variation of that veritable protestant ethic was often times crude and an atrocious naiveté to say the least. We constantly mistook conspicuous consumption for capitalist accumulation and reproduction. I have learned that you, Mr. Doe, had vowed to stage a boxing match with Colonel Ghaddafi in defense of these "pristine" ideals. But might there now be the need to distinguish these ideals from a grand ideology of Pax Americana? This is just a thought for consideration and soul searching. It is a thought to consider as we brace ourselves to embark upon a new frontier. For, it is about time that we examine our inner most consciences to see where and how we went wrong in the past. The goal is not to arrive at some preeminent and unified theory of political behavior that would pass as universal truths. But rather it must be, as someone indicated here today, a process of departures from errors in the search for norms of appropriateness, as we discern what ought to be in the universe of choices.

Amos Sawyer [1990-1994]: There are many foundational challenges that face us as we embark upon a new frontier of social change and civic accountability. The chaotic state of our economy and public administration can be addressed within the framework of constitutional reform. We attempted in the 1980s but there are not enough gains I can point to on this front. My fears are that we may repeat the mistakes of the past if enough gains are not made in revisiting some of the unsettled issues of the past. The unsettling constitutional dispensation happens to be one of those issues.

Samuel Doe [1980-1990]: I thought I commissioned you to reform our constitution during my tenure? Why was that task not completed in the 1980s when it should have been. I may be inclined now to think that perhaps attempts at tinkering with the current constitutional arrangement may not be necessary. Maybe the current constitutional framework may not be suited to our current conditions. I would take a radical approach now that we live in new historical realities. Perhaps, the particularities of our essential conditions call for a new constitutional dispensation in the establishment of new orders.

Amos Sawyer [1990-1994]: There was the constitutional drafting committee, and then, there was the constitutional assembly. These were two distinct undertakings and aspirations that I would view as being at cross-purposes. We were trying to end military rule while the assembly was interested in prolonging it. These are two distinct aspirations that were not only inherently contradictory, but were also mutually exclusive. They both coexisted in an explosive and potentially combustible political environment. In the end the constitutional assembly won because you remained in power beyond 1985.

Wilton Sankawulo [1995-1996]: I hear what you have to say but I will now turn to matters of economic policy. There has never been a forward-looking agrarian policy throughout the history of this commonwealth. But now necessity demands that the future path to economic development must first and foremost be rooted in the rural sector. The rural sector and the growth of a service sector should ensure linkages and structural mobility through the creation of jobs and services in other sectors. This is presumably what economists would refer to as the Keynesian multiplier effect (see Blinder, 1986). In the past, such outcomes were never the case because of the crowding out effect that the urban bias had on other sectors and regions. We must be very careful about setting up agricultural cooperatives, especially if they should be carried out on an involuntary basis.

There are threats of totalitarianism that must be avoided! There is always the need for an open mind on matters of cardinal principles such as these! For, agricultural cooperatives have proved to be somewhat sluggish in Eastern Europe and China in adapting to the dynamics of institutional and structural elements. These invariably include the demands of innovation, organizational change and productivity growth. This is while the collectives have been abandoned in Eastern Europe in the wake of market reforms and are being gradually abandoned in China in the new conditions of "capitalist realism." Similarly, the existence of a market infrastructure was absent in the Stalinist model in the East and that was one of many reasons for its undoing. There are, therefore, no guarantees that such agrarian philosophy is going to work in Liberia. There is always the middle, and, there are always the extremes in these matters. Western capitalism failed in the 1930s because of the false belief in the fetishism of automatic equilibrium and market clearing.

What was essentially ignored here with practical consequences was the plausibility of market failures. This idea of automatic market clearing in the classical and neo-classical systems was rooted in the moral philosophy and deductive methodology of Adam Smith, and perhaps other pre-classical sources in the history of political economy. It was not until Keynes' ideas came along forming a consensus in the middle ground before we knew that a permanent state of underemployment equilibrium in the form of depressed output conditions is a feasible scenario, where uncertainty regarding expectations and investment decisions is ubiquitous. Exploring the nature of uncertainty and its impact on market stability was significant. It was indeed, the epistemic dimension, which was for long overlooked in the orthodoxy of the Pre-Keynesian era in macro and micro theorizing.

Thus, voluntary cooperation should always be encouraged as a fact of life among rural farmers and dwellers. But cooperative endeavors in the rural economy must not be without the existence of a market infrastructure to connect buyers and sellers, taste, expectations and investment decisions. As with other aspects of national policy, this can take place within the context of a strategic framework of national priorities and policy preferences as a way of pursuing the middle path. There must be a reasonable degree of clarity on this issue because social cohesion and national security are impossible without economic and structural change to guarantee material well-being. If these were not the facts, then perhaps the tenor of our discourse and its theory could have been different. These are my views but I am by no means absolute that they are right. I am not so sure because I sometimes act or make utterances against my best instincts like everybody else. Is this the conduct of a reasonable person?

Ruth Perry [1996-1997]: Our discussion here today has great value in terms of taking stock and setting some parameters for our critical dialogue for the future. Through conversations like these we can achieve a lot on the path to reconstruction and national reconciliation. Through frank conversations like these we can gain greater wisdom in diagnosing the causes of political autocracy in our community. Bohm and his Associates (1991p.5; also quoted in chapter one) have shared the following words with us on the benefits of what I would call critical conversations:

> "Dialogue, as we are choosing to use the word, is a way of exploring the roots of the many crises that face humanity today. It enables inquiry into, and understanding of, the sorts of processes that fragment and interfere with real communication between individuals, nations and even different parts of the same organization. In our modern culture men and women are able to interact with one another in many ways: they can sing, dance or play together with little difficulty but their inability to talk together about subjects that matter deeply to them seems invariably to lead to dispute, division and often violence. In our view this condition points to a deep and pervasive defect in the processes of human thought."

Edwin Barclay [1930-1944]: I want to come back to the point Mr. Tolbert has made about the notion of fallibility, because I am inclined to think that it has formed the conceptual framework of our deliberations at this gathering. Indeed, the lesson of falibilism is that we proceed not towards truth but away from errors. We do so because we are more likely to know when we are wrong than when we are right. But why is this the case? It is so because we are willing to accept imperfections and incompleteness as per the epistemological status of our understanding. Our willingness to do this through the exercise of judgment is what distinguishes us as reasonable actors on the historical stage. Jack Mezirow (1998) refers to subjective reframing and our willingness to tentatively accept a best judgment in the absence of empirical evidence of the truth of a belief or an assertion.

Burbules (ibid) calls this exercise of judgment the pragmatic spirit. Bringing this process of exercising judgment to a logical conclusion would allow us to see that we may have taken actions in the past that went against our best instincts.[8] It would also allow us as leaders to atone for the injuries our actions or assertions may have caused others, and herein lies the path to humility and openness to new perspectives.

The path to openness and reason must engender reflection and critical introspection, and, eventually new interpretations, regarding the most profound issues of national reconstruction and social change. This new interpretative framework must seek to justify the need for atonement and some institutional means to avenge egregious violations of humanitarian principles during the years of conflict. I essentially agree with a Liberian author when he expressed the following sentiments in a poem underscoring our collective national failures for the past generation:

The Beginning of our Time

The beginning of our time
Once upon a time there were sounds of gunshots
Once upon a time the morning was short

The not so timid sun intercepted with less than usual vehemence
We were told that day would be memorable
We were told that a new chronicle in the pages of history had began
We were told that the time of the people had come

It seems there was feeling of excitement
How sweet were the songs of enchantment
How short our new heavens had lasted
How fickle our new heroes were
The almost broken stick was stronger that this tide
But there was also a feeling of leaping into the unknown
I can now say where have we been?
My God, was this the beginning of time again?
A new time that would see the long walk and thirst and great longing
for food and other simpler amenities and basics of life

The story began with a big bang
Heard about that other explanation
Of how the universe began?
Everyone is hesitant to describe the whole dimensions
The Master Sergent turned Machiavellian, turned a bit of Nero,
turned a bit of all that is not so good and so kind in our midst

The self-proclaimed redeemer turned into a paradise lost and naked
promises
Promises we have heard a thousand times
Remember the times?

The roosters have not come home to roost
The children of the universe deserve their justice!
Someone once said Liberia was like a mosaic
That for it to blossom, all its different colors must be made manifest
Is that the destiny of a people so long neglected by their land folks?

Perhaps this is all in the past now
Perhaps there are better days ahead
The earth must move for everything else to move
Hopefully this will happen
Perhaps not so sudden but once again as always
The earth will move!
The power of the sun will make us move
The power of Africa's sun

Garrestson W. Gibson [1900-1904]: You are right I find it difficult to
query your positions. I am convinced that your thoughts may be rooted
in the very nature of human rationality. I should submit that there are
many calculations that go into our decision-making processes. These
include our prejudices, ambitions, fears and other considerations in
the metaphysical realms. I for instance now think that the introduction
of the hut tax was not only a pernicious error of judgment, but it was
driven by prejudice and sheer discrimination against the indigenes.
Why wasn't the tax a universal or progressive tax for example? We could
have raised money to show up our frequently dismal fiscal position
through a system of progressive taxation in the land. Furthermore, the
manner in which our bureaucracy administered that tax by applying
autocratic methods through the liberal use of the Frontier Force to inflict
unnecessary violence was mind bugling. This was an ugly experience in
the annals of our fiscal history that should never be repeated as we look
forward to a better future!

I am of the opinion that there is only one future in Liberia and that is a future in a polycentric social order. Autocracy and the untold damages caused by personal power have made it abundantly clear that multiple centers of decision making that affect the most varied aspects of our lives is the only logical path to prosperity and sustainable peace. A polycentric social order in Liberia will involve strengthening civil society and guaranteeing individual rights through the formation of countervailing social structures to enhance the functional capabilities of the state. It will ultimately involve overarching behavioral and institutional change. Because it has become all too clear that the necessary and sufficient conditions for achieving these lofty ideals consist in the willingness of most of our compatriots to accept and become a part of a change process.

Alfred F. Russell [1883-1884]: I wish to thank everyone who has come to our palaver hut to participate in this discussion. It has been the most gracious opportunity of a lifetime. The most basic paradox about the Liberian condition is that a society, which was conceived on the basis of a messianic purpose to be a safe haven for liberty and the downtrodden, turned out to be a natural habitat for the rise of autocracy. Anyway, this has been probably one of the most productive sessions in the history of our social and political life. I view our gathering here today as the high point of civil dialogue as we arise out of the ashes of national decay. Quite frankly speaking, there has never been a time as far back as I can remembered when we, the past and present leaders of this suffering nation, have come together to discuss in such a fashion.

I am convinced that this action will have a lasting impact on posterity and our current efforts to right the numerous wrongs of the past. We have discussed almost everything from economics, culture, principles of morality and ethics to politics etc. We have further attempted to come to terms with the very nature of human rationality and action. We have recognized through our various arguments and counterarguments, the need for openness in our perennial search for a more rational order of society. The quintessential conclusion I have drawn from these deliberations is that our actions must always be tempered by the fact that the certainty of the information and knowledge we have can never be said to be absolute, especially in the realms of reason and secular activity. You are welcome lady and gentlemen! Oh! My palm whine cup is emptied is anyone interested in a refill?

IV
"Barbarism or Civilization in the way ahead?"

This section looks at other dimensions that I have not already discussed in terms of the underlying causes of the breakdown of order and civility in the Liberian society. The situation in Liberia today demands that the social analyst must revisit the most profound and unresolved aspects pertaining to some of the debates that took place at the beginning of state formation in the middle of the 19th century. As the last section has demonstrated, it would be impossible to move ahead without an attempt to revisit the past and put things into their proper historical perspectives and causal frameworks.

This section is also a narrative about the reasons for hope and a possibility of social transformation in a land of false starts and numerous chances. After more than 150 years of national existence, the vision and task of building a black civilization based on order and a distinctive national consciousness remain elusive. In undertaking this task, we must proceed armed with our openness, permeable and inclusive perspectives within the context of transformation. We must proceed with the emotional readiness and tenacity to anticipate organizational and structural change.

Thus, it is significant to elaborate upon the relationship between the assimilationist ideology of Hilary Teage (1840s) or of C. L. Simpson (1960s) and state failure in Liberia. The assimilitionist ideology of Hilary Teage was propagated in the spirit of the French revolution of 1789 and the European enlightenment—which proclaimed a superior western civilization that Africa was admonished to aspire to (see Dunn and Tarr, 1985). But with what degrees of confidence could one argue that our failure to build a nation at ease with itself results from the earlier "consensus" among a core of repatriate political rulers? A consensus that suggested that assimilation was better than integration within the orbit of Liberian society.

159

What is the meaning of civilization within the particularistic Liberian context? And to what extent have our attempts to uncritically assimilate the historical and cultural experiences of the West resulted in a miserable failure? How can we deconstruct the ahistoricism and some of the myths about the lack of vitality and pertinence of African culture? How could we possibly do this in a deliberate attempt to fashion a new interpretive framework amenable to the challenges of a modern epoch? These are some of the issues that have preoccupied and seized my attention in this section. I will provide some clues to the aforementioned questions departing from the lessons of history, tradition, culture and transactional relations between the socio-historical entities that came to constitute the Liberian polity over the span of many decades.

A theory of history and social progress

For over 15 decades the Liberian experiment in development or social progress has been a tortured one. This is not to suggest that this noble enterprise at historical progress could be deemed as being humanly impossible. Such assumptions would be further from the truth. There is no other way to describe them. This great historic mission to unlock the mysteries of progress cannot be deemed as a fiat accompli indeed. For to argue that would amount to ignoring the general trend of historical progress over many years of existence, which leads to more enlightenment and not less, albeit often in a nonlinear fashion. As when we saw a total breakdown of any semblance of civilization under the aegis of national socialism in Hitler's Germany in the 1930s and 40s.

The general trend of historical progress leads to new and improved ways of being, centering belief systems, validation, cognition and the elaboration of more complex and conceptual principles of action. It inexorably leads to the development of economic and institutional rationalization and cultural foundations. Progress leads to the development of social relations and the refinement of techniques that enable harmonious coexistence and all forms of democratic pluralism. Progress further leads to the development and refinement of constitutional frameworks to regulate economic exchange and monitor the perversion of society by putting breaks on all forms of deviance that challenge our notions and commitment to a moral heritage. It also leads to the regulation of all forms of authority and the bureaucratic system so that they may become enablers not fetters on the further development of individuals, civil society and the state system.

The tendencies of historical progress have led to the formation of universalist ideals such as liberty, solidarity and the notion of natural rights. It has led to the unprecedented accentuation of agency and new articulations of global forces in the spheres of social and economic relations. These tendencies or processes of becoming have seamlessly seen the withering away of the old and the coming into being of the new in accordance with governing laws and principles of history and nature. Frederick Engels (p.3) is very eloquent on this notion of change and continuity in his treatise on Feuerbach:

> ...Truth lay now in the process of cognition itself, in the long historical development of science, which mounts from lower to ever higher levels of knowledge without ever reaching, by discovering absolute truth, a point at which it can proceed no further, where it would have nothing more to do than to fold its hands and gaze with wonder at the absolute truth it has attained. And what holds good for the realm of philosophical knowledge holds good also for that of every other kind of knowledge and also for practical action. Just as knowledge is unable to reach a complete conclusion in a perfect, ideal condition of humanity, so is also history unable to do so; a perfect society, a perfect "state", are things which can only exist in the imagination."

The process of historical development is always imperfect as are the categories of thought and action. I am inclined to emphasize that it took the West thousands of years from the Greek city-states, the Magna Carta in 1215 to the continental United States, to give us what we today perceive as liberal democracy. Even at that, only a few would argue that liberal democracy among the Anglo Saxons, Asians, and Germanic peoples is not vastly a work in progress. Who would argue against the fact that the constitutional monarchy in Japan is at most imperfect? Who would also argue against the presumption that liberal or capitalist democracy, by canonizing the logic of competition engendered the worst forms of colonial exploitation and plantation slavery? Cultural and historical imperfections are facts of life because they powerfully reflect the unsettling nature of human reality.

But cultural, institutional and historical imperfections do not signal preordained cataclysms and uncontrollable disruptions in the path to a humane and civic order. Not even in Liberia, which has seen too much chaos in these last 14 years. What one must realize is the existence of potentialities and possibilities as ontological facts. In effect, the theory of chaos as one might express through the dialectical law of the unity of opposites is also a theory about the constitution of order. This assertion is predicated upon an understanding of the imperatives of practical reason in the explanation of history and society. It is an understanding of chaos that suggests that where there is chaos and barbarism, there is every possibility for the emergence of social order and civilization. And no human society is exempted from the workings of this null hypothesis. There is often dualism and multiple features of a given social and cultural system. Thus, the existence of dualism within the very nature of Liberian society is an empirical fact.

Dualism as a constitutive variable suggests that in Liberia, you have a modern sector of education and socialization complimented by a traditional sector that carry out more or less similar functions in specific cognitive and conative domains. These two sectors tend to interact negatively or positively pending on the nature and structure of the interaction. Thus in this formulation one views a symmetry between order and civilization on the one hand, and chaos and barbarism on the other. Another way of looking at this formulation is to evoke the basic propositions of Hegelian logic. This concerns the logic of an identity condition that postulates that two contradictory phenomena may have the same referent but a different mode of presentation. Michel Foucault (1961) refers to this as the hermeneutic conundrum from which we can conclude that the accepted notion of reason can be defined by the negative qualities of unreason. The challenge of virtually recreating the Liberian state and all its social and authority systems in the face of great historic failures consists in this singular realization. What is important here to note is that all societies go through social change and how they manage or mismanage such change makes a difference between being in a state of barbarism or a state of civilization and social order.

The search for civilization and social order

Throughout history mankind has always sought for the most optimal system that engenders a sense of community and shared identity. In the history of humans the transition from hunter-gatherer to communal and civic consciousness was a remarkable process and achievement. I would argue that there was a seed of progress rooted in the very nature of human cognition and social reality that would facilitate this process. Never in the evolution of our social consciousness could one envision that this seed of progress would come to bare fruits thousands of years ago. The germination of this seed inexorably led to the dawn of civilization and the consolidation of forms of order. We have also seen higher forms of cognition and linguistic consciousness, and their attendant social and historical contradictions, as we perceive them to be. All these natural and socio-historical contours have solidified the movement of human beings since the dawn of civilization to more complex and elaborate forms of understanding of cause and effect, order and civility.

This process of the search for order or normal existence has been crystallized both in the temporal and spiritual dimensions of human existence and essences from antiquity up to present. We see this in the so-called primordial forms of religion. We see it also in the more systematic and rational theologies as well as mythologies of the ancient Hebrews of Western Asia and inhabitants of the Indian subcontinent. We also see this attempt to impose spiritual order on a chaotic universe through the teachings of Jesus Christ as handed down to us through the canonical gospels and the Gnostic tradition. In their attempts to impose order and explain the origins of the universe, the ancient Egyptians held that the universe evolved from chaotic matter, which was in essence the equivalent of non-being (see Diop, 1991).

This is a concept of the evolution of matter and its manifestations from being created in potentiality to being created in actuality. All matter are said to be created in potentiality before being created in actuality, which is the same as in Plato's "the Same and the Other" the theory of reminiscences, etc. or Aristotle's matter and privation, potentiality and actuality etc. (ibid). The materialist component of Egyptian thought would also later prevailed among the Greek and Latin Atomists, Democratus, Epicurus and Lucretius (ibid).

We see that the Egyptian cosmogony is materialistic up to this point by professing a materialist stance when postulating the existence of an uncreated matter, "excluding nothingness and containing its own principle of evolution as an intrinsic property" (ibid, p.311). However, with the appearance of the demiurge or Ra the cosmogony of ancient Egypt takes on a new dimension with the infusion of an idealist component. In this new cosmological framework, Ra achieves creation through the word as in the objective idealism of Hegel or the Judeo-Christian paradigms (ibid). Indeed, in the book of Genesis Moses says "in the beginning God created the heaven and the earth. And the earth was without form, or void; and darkness was upon the face of the deep. And the Spirit of God moved upon the face of the waters. And God said let there be light: and there was light." (Genesis, 1:1-3). Thus in this formulation the universe is created through the word and not from the category of potentiality. It is created from a state of nothingness. This explanation is to demonstrate the antecedent or parenthood of Egyptian and African civilization in terms of subsequent evolutions in the varying fields of intellectual and social thought especially in classical times. Hence, the indelible imprints of Africa on all of classical scholarship and religious thought is historically self-evident.

Citing passages from a poem published by Hiliary Teage in 1842, the first President of Liberia, Joseph Jenkins Roberts, proclaimed in a speech to the Liberia Lyceum in 1845 (see Burrowes, 1998, p.37):

> Here science once displayed
> And art their charms!
> Here awful pharaohs swayed
> Great nations who obeyed;
> Here distant monarchs laid
> Their vanquished arms.

John Henrik Clarke (see Diop, 1991) has suggested how great masterpieces of Egyptian history was for a long time deliberately ignored by mainstream western historians in their bid to construct the false assumption that Egyptian civilization was white. These works include but not limited to the following (ibid): Gerald Massey's great classic, Ancient Egypt: The Light of the World (1907); Politics, Intercourse, and Trade of the Carthaginians and Ethiopians by A. Heereen (1833) and The Ruins of Empire by Count C. F. Volney (1787).

In his work, Egypt, Sir E.A. Willis Budge comments (ibid, p. xix):

The prehistoric native of Egypt, both in the old and new stone Age, was African, and there is every reason for saying that the earliest settlers came from the South.

He further goes on to comment:

There are many things in the manners and customs and religions of the historic Egyptians that suggest that the original home of their ancestors was in a country in the neighborhood of Uganda and Punt.

In the realms of social and objective existence, we know that we cannot proceed with the requisite certainty within a class system or a system of power and social relations, without a profound sense or some degree of confidence in the stability of the social order. This social order or normal forms of existence or what I would civilization is often challenge by the lack of equilibrium between private and public interests in the most varying social systems. This lack of equilibrium can lead to chaos, social revolutions or the dethroning of the earlier civilization. Max Weber has captured this process in terms of the nature of power and forms of authority through ideal types as standard analytical constructs.

The consequences of the breakdown of order come to life through the imaginations of William Shakespeare in one of his numerous plays and poems. In Shakespeare's Troilus and Cressida written shortly after Hamlet (1600-1601); Ulysses speaks of the ideal natural order while at the same time plotting to employ stratagems based on the realities of power. In Ulysses world, power has become the center of everything.

Shakespeare tells us that the trappings of his perceived might within the social order blind Ulysses, but it is this blindness that ultimately leads to his undoing. In this play we read a process of ascendance or an allegory that speaks to the dark side of power especially when it is abused and misused. Recent Liberian history tells us a thing or two about the decomposition of power within a social order especially when its primary nature and limits are misperceived. The downfall of the True Whig Party, Doe regime, and of the Taylor regime reveals that blatant disregard for the rule of law by erecting illigitimate structures of domination does not last long. It can be only a passing fad and it has tremendous consequences for the building of social order and a civilization.

The lesson to draw from these episodes is that all illigimate forms of authority that are constituted outside a popular consensus are doomed to fail. This is the Liberian historical experience. I would assume that the decomposition of such authority is occasioned by the very logic of the process of rationalization and enlightenment in history. Weber has commented on this question of the dissolution of illegitimate authority as we can see in the remark by Parkin (1982,p.75):

> "Weber was most aware than most that the history of political systems was not exactly a chronicle of the affections displayed by the lowly towards their masters. His assumption seems to have been that regimes cannot exist by coercion alone, and that some degree of moral support from below is necessary to the long term survival of any authority system…Regimes that fail to establish such claims are presumably distained for the rubbish-tip of history."

The process of personal transformation

This sub-section concludes that the path to national reconstruction in Liberia lies in critical consciousness and participatory democracy. The conclusion is supportive of previous assumptions in the book. This conclusion in a very fundamental way constitutes also the underlying foundation of my arguments in this book. It constitutes the core and nerve center of my views, which have been forming for the past four years. Hence, the section conforms the essential maxim that through personal transformation, human beings can become better and improved actors on the historical stage in terms of the quality of their insights and actions. Consequently, the article calls for the formation of a cultural synthesis, which extols the practical value of personal and social transformation imbedded within Liberian culture.

The sub-section is also a critical account about some of the underlying psychological and social determinants of action that have led to the breakdown of order and civility in the Liberian society. It is also a narrative about the reasons for hope and a possibility of social transformation in a land that has witnessed so much chaos in a generation. After more than 150 years of national existence, the vision and task of building a black civilization on the west coast of Africa based on order and a distinctive national consciousness remain elusive. The situation in Liberia today demands that the social analyst must reexamine established norms; social practices and institutional patterns that took shaped and persisted since the beginning of state formation in the middle of the 19th century. It is possible that such undertaking would lead to more holistic and permeable perspectives that legitimate the aspirations for social change.

The process of social and institutional change in Liberia must be anchored in personal transformation and collective empowerment. It must occur in the cognitive and affective domains of conscious historical and social actors especially adults. For, it is adults who primarily heads state and private institutions, schools, colleges and who can become political and social leaders in the society. They must provide guidance and set trends as such that society would become amendable to change for the better if adults would also become amendable to change. Change in Liberia especially at the institutional and civic level encapsulates cognitive processes that are mediated by collective cultural norms and psychosocial assumptions (see Mezirow, 1981; 2000).

At the heart of this process of social transformation is the attainment of critical consciousness at the individual and collective levels. Salomon (1993,p.xiii) has spoken to this issue by positing that:

"People appear to think in conjunction or partnership with others and with the help of culturally provided tools that are brought to bear on this or that problem; rather, they emerge in a situation tackled by teams of people and tools available to them...What characterizes such daily events of thinking is that the social and artifactual surrounds, alleged to be outside the individual's heads, not only are sources of stimulation and guidance but are actually vehicles of thought. Moreover, the arrangements, functions, and structures of these surrounds change in the process to become genuine parts of the learning that results from the cognitive partnership with them. In other words, it is not just the person-solo who learns, but the person-plus, the whole system of interrelated factors".

Brookfield (1993,pp.10-11) has intimated that "in a critical conversion, we seek to locate our private troubles in the context of public issues, while considering forms of collective action in different situations that might change individual histories. We then reflect on the appropriateness of these forms of action and on how we might learn from our experience as we reenter the domain of action."

He further goes on to elaborate that (p.11):
"The reunification between the personal and political, the individual and collective, is the focus of the condition of communitarianism. This condition urges participants in critical conversation to search for common elements in seemingly idiosyncratic experiences and to discover common interests as a basis for collective action."

The attainment of critical consciousness as an instrumental objective in organizational and institutional processes in Liberia is undergirded by assumptions, which depart from a theory of motivation that is concerned with conscious experience, the full range of emotions and the self (see Weiner, 1989). This theory of motivation is also primarily concerned with deciphering the meaning of an action (ibid, p.7). A theory of motivation concerned with conscious experience and the meaning of an action reinforces phenomenological perspectives that speak to the importance of our diverse perceptions of reality.

Politics and the development of consciousness

The exercise of politics like other domains of social endeavors suggests that it is also the product of consciousness. We generate our strategies and tools, symbols and mental models for problem solving from within our minds both intuitively and rationally. Contemporary neurological research conforms the place and centrality of consciousness in our conscious actions and learning. Gustavsson and Harung (1994,p.1) have indicated that "previous research indicate that there are a number of distinct stages of psychological development of an individual's consciousness, and that the level of development has a direct bearing on a person's perception of reality and his ability to perform—professionally and socially." Consciousness in this heuristic context is therefore the source of most human failings and misconceived actions, and yet the source of all happiness and personal and social well being.

I have argued that the gateway to social change in Liberia requires a foundational and radical transformation in our consciousness both individually and collectively (Johnson, 2003). The object of such transformation is to attain critical consciousness. My central message in critical analysis for the past four years in the particular fields of learning and social action is that our frames of reference, which underguide our thoughts and actions, are determined by our consciousness. I see the role of consciousness as one, which might alternatively energize or corrode the enterprise of recreating the Liberian state. Thus in this vein it is reasonable to affirm that at the heart of the challenge of national renewal lays a critical awareness, reflection and other categories of communicative learning. Habermas has underscored the importance of discourse in his theory of communicative action. In Habermas' conception of communicative rationality, all state power derives from the communicative power of its citizens (see Johnson, 2002). This suggests that rational discourse and the consensual validation of norms and institutional patterns are indispensable to the building of a viable social democracy within a national polity.

Relying upon Mead's ideas of mindedness, Goff noted that the capacity for critical reflection requires a developed mind and life experiences (Haddad, 2003). Mead intimates that the initial development of the mind and our sense of self, which develops through social interaction, must begin by internalizing existing knowledge structures (ibid, p.53). As such the existing meanings and social arrangements into which each child is born become part of the earliest definitions of self and world. For social transformation to occur Goff noted that the actor must not only actively protest against internalized images and ideas about reality and self, but must also communicate this to others and engage in the difficult task of convincing others to oppose accepted definitions of self.

This conclusion to me is the challenge of both activism and scholarship in Liberia today. We must develop appropriate institutions to arrest the process of alienation, which is so pervasive among the youth and many of our current factional and rebel leaders. Alienation and chronic illiteracy are the two most corrosive factors that undermine the forging of a collective national consciousness. In a rather curious way one could postulate that alienation is a source of selfishness because it leads to a lack of hope in the principle of common destiny and collective interdependence.

Goff (ibid, p.53) has further proposed that in order to understand how reified structures predominate over reflexivity based in praxis, analysts should examine the extent to which structural arrangements isolate individuals from direct and lived experiences that challenge reified structures. Such structural arrangements are manifested in formal institutions of socialization (such as schools and religious institutions) that transmit values outside concrete structures in which they have meaning and in institutionalized structural arrangements that serve to separate individuals into small cliques that isolate them from larger communal realities and interests. What such process of alienation from communal realities does is that the interest of the few becomes placed above the interest of society. Parochial notions of protecting the interest of the tribe as we sometimes saw during the war in Liberia becomes more important in such situations then the interest of the nation. The interest of the self becomes antithetical to the interests of the other.

Constructive developmental theory sheds light on the cognitive process that leads to personal transformation. It suggests that a form of knowing always consists of the relationship or temporary equilibrium between the subject and the object. This is a developmental process by which what was subject in our knowing becomes an object. This is the same as transformational learning because it focuses on the process of meaning becoming clarified (Mezirow, 2003). It leads to greater control over thinking, feeling and will (ibid). It makes the actor to become more reflective in their decision making so that they may act when it becomes feasible (ibid).

The subject-object relationship always forms the core of an epistemology (Kegan, 2000). The object describes the thoughts and feelings we have. The subject refers to the thoughts and feelings that we cannot separate from. It is those thoughts and feelings that exist within us (ibid). The process of development of consciousness becomes a process of transformation of subject into object in terms of our ways of knowing and validation (ibid). Such transformation can be reflected in all aspects of our lives including politics, professional commitment and the commitment to one's family and community. There is a famous late 19th century literary example of transformation adapted by Robert Kegan (ibid, pp.54-57) from the closing scene of Ibsen's Doll's House.

What the exchange in the adaptation of the play suggests is that the main character Nora is not just changing her mind in the sense that she is becoming less persuaded by formerly held ideas and beliefs and more persuaded by an emerging set of ideas. She is coming to a new set of ideas about her ideas, about the sources of these ideas, about who authorizes them or make them true. In effect, Nora is rejecting her identification with prior assumptions, feelings and beliefs as given truths. The forms of knowing that gave rise to her beliefs have been transformed from external identification to internal authority (ibid, p.58-59). It is this type of cognitive transformation in a person that is synonymous with critical awareness or critical consciousness.

Critical consciousness leads to a change in our frames of reference or meaning structures by making us critically award of why our assumptions have come to constrain the way we perceive, understand and feel about our world (Johnson, 2002). It is to all intents and purposes the antecedent or a necessary condition for self-determination and objective social empowerment. This type of consciousness evidently stands in contradistinctions to false consciousness. Geuss (as cited in Mezirow, 1985,p.145) for example, has identified false consciousness as a falsely perceived ideology that fosters dependency relationships through the force of tradition and external identification.

Secular and spiritual aspects of personal transformation

This sub-section seeks to elaborate on the secular and spiritual dimensions of traditional systems and methods of socialization in Liberia. There are elements of personal and social transformation within these systems that have been used for many generations to secure order and civilization. What is important to stress, however, is that these methods of personal and social transformations can be misappropriated pending on the predispositions and ideological orientations of political and social agents. In 1991 at the height of the civil war in Liberia—Cuttington University College administrator Henrique Tokpa made this observation about the behavior of young rebel fighters on the Cuttington Campus during the early stages of the war (1991p.87):

> "Many of the men wore wedding gowns, wigs, dresses, commencement gowns from high schools, and several forms of 'voodoo' regalia. All rebels wore cotton strings around the wrist and around the neck and shoulder. They all displayed black tattoos on the arm, slightly below the shoulder. They believed that any person who wore these talismans and tattoos, and strictly adhered to the laws of not eating, pumpkin, having sex, touching lime and taking bath, could not be killed in battle by enemy fire. Because of the importance of this 'bullet proof' protection, there was a medicine man in residence at the Cuttington training base to administer these medicines at the end of their military training."

These recruits had undergone a process of ritual initiation typical of traditional initiation schools that stress the symbolic nature of ritual as a minesfitation of the transformation of children into adulthood. The process of transformation has both secular and spiritual implications in the initiation schools or societies particularly those of the Poro. Apart from the educational and spiritual track, both the Poro and Sande also have a political dimension. They have served as stabilizing elements whose religious and social control were conducive to maintaining public order in the pre and post republican era in Liberia. The Poro since its emergence around the sixteenth century has displayed amazing flexibility and "capacity for accommodation, seeking often to validate adaptations and thereby securing its continuing legitimacy." (Sawyer, 1992,p.50).

Sawyer (ibid) citing d'Azevedo has intimated that the Poro "provided a sacred and secret arm of political authority and intergroup diplomacy that helped to maintain stability through appeal to the gerontocratic and hierarchical principles derived from the ideal model of the ranked-lineage structure." The Sande has been used as an instrument to inculcate modern conceptions of maternity and childcare as well as traditional ones. But what is of significance in this section is the role of the Poro as an instrument of personal and social transformation. This developmental process of change into adulthood is also usually perceived as a person entering the spirit world and returning to his comminunity as a new being.

One distinguishing characteristic of people undergoing such experience is that they are regarded as being potententially dangerous because they do not fit into a specific category of behavior (Ellis, 1997). Elias Canetti (cited in Ellis, 1997) has described this state of being as one of a liminal condition. This liminal condition is exceptional in that "it is often marked by ritual drama, which is in effect an attempt to manage change through religion." The liminal condition is an intermediate zone of identity transformation. It is highly delicate and therefore many things can go wrong when it is poorly managed as we saw in the case of the terrible atrocities that were committed by adolescent boys while dressed in women's clothing.

Ellis (ibid) has addressed the distinctive dress style of initiates as a symbolic feature of the elements of spiritual and ontological transformations. Young rebels wearing such regalia are saying that they are going through an intermediate zone of transition and therefore they are dangerous. What is important to note here is how the warring factions in Liberia from the 1990s up to present, have misused the rituals of initiation of our traditional societies to their selfish ends. There is the reality or mystique of the diving king that speaks to how symbols of the Poro have been misappropriated for the wrong reasons. The divine king is the one who directs the transformation of others but he by all accounts is not subject to self-transformation. And herein lies the mystique of his powers- he changes others but he cannot change (ibid). In other words, he has unlimited powers to determine the rules of the game while at the same time not subject to those rules. Canetti (see ibid) believes that the figure of the divine king has had a decisive influence on our modern conception of power in that the state could easily usurp the powers of the divine king. The divine king in the context of conflicts in Liberia and West Africa could be a rebel leader (Charles Taylor, Ahiji Kromah, Sekou Conneh) or the zoes hired by them to do their biding.

At the end of the process of transformation or rite of passage occasioned by the Poro is rebirth whereby a person becomes born again. The expectation of this new person is to be reintegrated into society on the basis of the new outlook. This process of transformation in consciousness is not dissimilar to a Christian conversion experience. In this particular regards Ellis (1999,p.268) remands us that there were in fact many instances of Christian conversions during the course of the war, particularly in the 1990s:

> "It appears that Christian teaching is particularly attractive to any ex-fighter who wishes to make a radical break with his or her past, perhaps because of the Christian belief that the Holy Spirit is universal in nature and can enter anybody to provide instant transformation. One eleven year-old former fighter, for example, having been 'born-again' in Christ, said he had 'taken an oath never to kill again. Certainly, a number of former fighters, including such leading fighters as Blahyi, Milton and Armah Youlo, claimed to have become born-again Christians."

The Poro rite of passage is also akin to other modern and secular concepts of personal transformation in some respects. For example, the last stage of Mezirow's perspective transformation involves the reintegration into society on the basis of the conditions dictated by the new perspective or critical consciousness (see Mezirow, 2000). This critical consciousness, which in this context is the educational and cognitive goal of perspective transformation makes one a productive member of a civilization and a more civically responsible person opened to new perspectives and change. Labouvie-Vief (cited in Johnson, 2003) believed that one of the structural transitions of adulthood was to achieve new integration in which initially de-contextualized logic was to become re-embedded in its social context. An example of perspective transformation through critical reflection can be cited at work in the mind of the African Patriot Nelson Mandela (Mezirow, 2000,p.57):

"I was struck most forcefully by the discrepancy between my old assumptions and my actual experience. I had discarded my presumptions that graduates automatically became leaders and that my connection to the Thembu royal house guaranteed me respect. Having a successful career and a comfortable salary were no longer my ultimate goals. I found myself being drawn into the world of politics because I was not content with my old beliefs."

Below is another example of perspective transformation of one of the informants I worked with at a local college in Chicago in 2003:

"Going to college has allowed me to grow up in a way that I never expected. I used to have a short temper but I no longer have that. Everything I am learning in college has helped me to see things in a different way. I apply what I am learning to solve real life problems and that is great."

In my extensive interviews with another informant who had just recently arrived in the United States from Liberia, he informed me that he was force to reexamine some of the deeply held taken-for- granted assumptions he had about life and pursuing a career in Liberia:

175

"Before I left Liberia for advanced studies in Europe in the late 1980s, I thought that I could one day return with a law degree and earned a comfortable living practicing law in Liberia. But no sooner then I returned with an advanced degree in Law in the late 1990s, then I began to realize that I had to change my assumptions. I saw that the legal system was broken and therefore I could not earned a comfortable living from practicing law in such environment. This change of mind first led to a moment of crisis, followed by a fervent desire to gain a new outlook in terms of my priorities and career prospects. I now believe that this life is not necessarily about how much I can get but about how much I can contribute toward the betterment of a society that has been thoroughly destroyed. I have decided to change my career and go into education where I may be able to influence and touch the lives of many, particularly the younger generation that has been robed their chances to succeed in our society."

Yet another informant from Liberia had this to say about the triggers of his perspective transformation around 1992, when the war in Liberia had been raging for about three years:

"The most significant trigger that led to a complete turn around in life was the death of my father at the hands of rebels in the early 1990s. The news of the death of my father, while I was already based in the United States led to a temporary crisis for me. My entire world was completely shattered at that moment. But I must admit that this crisis was good in a way because it forced me to put my life into proper perspective. It genuinely allowed me to step back and reevaluate my life up to that point. I was forced to reexamine previous assumptions. I realized that because of my father's death I would now be thrown into a leadership position within my family. Before the death of my father, it seemed that I was constantly drifting in various directions, not knowing what really to do with my life. But I started to become more focused and goal oriented, realizing that I now had a greater burden to carry in living up to the expectations of my late father. This to me was a real transformation in my way of thinking and living."

Although the volitional and rational nature of perspective transformation makes it different from the Poro initiation and its esoteric rituals, there are some similarities in terms of the educational and instrumental goals of all personal transformations in both the spiritual and secular domains. These educational values include respect and care for the elderly, consensus decision-making, openness to dialogue and change, collective action, compassion as well as respect for spiritual and duly constituted secular authority. Beryl L. Bellman (1984,pp.94-95) in his book the Language of Secrecy had some interesting exchanges with an informant regarding some aspects of the training that Poro society initiates undergo. During the exchange, when Mr. Bellman asked the informant about some of the laws and rules of behavior that Poro initiates must conform to, this is what he, the informant, had to say:

> "Like for a typical example, if I go back there and I get there, any of those boys see me, they have to bend down until I pass. That is the respect and the training they undergo. Two, when you are walking on the road and you find someone coming and you people are two walking, you go one side and they pass one side; they shouldn't pass between you because the person that has the bad luck carrying and he passes between you, it will stay on you. You see, these are the things. The next thing for respect, again because they are more likely teaching that they have to respect people on it, those are some of the things. If you see someone coming with a load on his or her head, you excuse the person's pass; you don't allow the person to get into the bush; you go to the side of the road and the person passes. And then you get there...The kind of things for respect? Like if I see any of my elder, some old Pa, uh, and I want to shake their hand, I take off my hat and I shake the person's hand. You see I don't leave the hat on and shake the person's hand. You see only a Poro man should do that. Like a typical example, when I am sitting, I see any of the old people, coming I get up and let them sit down. I am supposed to stand. When we are eating, I am supposed to hold the can with my hand and we eat."

The determinants of civilization in Liberia

Western education in Liberia is the most important criterion or component of civilization. But what this assumption ignores is that civilization as I am describing it predates western education. For example, the Babylonians, Nubians or ancient Ethiopians did not have a system of western education, as we know it and these are precisely the antecedents and sources of western civilization. A civilized man is also one who wears western dress and shoes and lives in a western styled house with western styled furniture in it (Moran, 1990). These are the outward signs of civilization in Liberia, which can be described at best as superficial. For, the business of civilization far transcends one's taste in clothes and shoes. There is also a gender construction of civilization, which in most instances works against the economic and social empowerment of women. Moran has stated (ibid, p.70) that "a civilized woman without an employed man, however, is in the unenviable position of being virtually unable to support herself and her children, and there are many in these straits who depend on relatives and boyfriends for a precarious existence."

One can see that in the past there was a system of acculturation whose basic premises and assumptions were wrong or at best problematic. Hence, where weak and blundering policies failed to accomplish acculturation, they created opportunities for exploitation by the ruling elites and their henchmen in the interior. However, President Arthur Barclay, like Blyden and John Payne Jackson had argued, tried to fashion a policy of government that would be amenable to the demands of an African setting. Barclay argued for wider and deeper culture and an intimate intercourse with indigenous culture (Johnson, 1987). Although the form and content of his approach may not have been properly conceptualized, it came closed to anything resembling a cultural synthesis as a blue print for social policy.

Today one can argue that the basic framework of this cultural synthesis places premium on the possibility of social and personal transformation—such as the hope and faith that human beings can become better and improved actors on the historical stage in terms of their thought and action. The basic logic imbedded in this assumption is that a civilized society is one, which manages all forms of transformations as a necessary and obligatory principle of self-preservation and achieving what I would call functional equilibrium. This is what at a deeper epistemological level the esoteric rituals of the Poro and Sande are all about. It is also what the rationalist tradition and perspective transformation in the corpus of adult development is all about.

The way ahead for Liberia

Today there is a complete breakdown of order in Liberia even as the current interim administration and the United Nations take some positive steps toward creating a new future. As I have already noted, the international community can play its part to change Liberia, but Liberians must be willing psychologically to facilitate this process. Thus, the fundamental question of which way we should proceed in building a viable and sustainable path to the future is purely a matter of enlightened choice. It is a choice to be made for civilization or barbarism as I have described them; it is a choice for anarchy or for a stable social order.

There is no doubt that the post-independence period in Liberia began with a false start as I have alluded to in the introductory section of this paper. Freepong (2003) has argued that one of the reasons for which Liberia failed to attained successful statehood was its inability to confront the crisis of identity at the beginning of its formation. He has suggested that this crisis of identity is one of several crises that must be resolved at the beginning of state formation (ibid). The author goes on to assert that by confronting this issue of cultural identity, people learn to identify themselves as citizens of the nation state, rather than as members of provincial entities and particular ethnic sub-groups.

Regrettably, the type of effort and existential exercise emphasized by Freepong was not successfully undertaken at the beginning in Liberia, but this task must now be reevaluated in approaching the future. This task involves new approaches, perspectives, consciousness, and a new pan ethnic civilization that values civil and communicative democracy and action. It also involves the creation of a new covenant with the Liberian people undergirded by a cultural synthesis that ensure economic security and the infusion of a moral purpose in the historical project of recreating the Liberian state. Thus the post war cultural situation must transcend the impediments of the old divisions and reified economic and social structures put in place by men who did not understand the finer details and vitality of African culture.

There are many policy and private decisions in the policy domain that will follow the building of a post civil war society in Liberia. The next administration must ensure actions and practices that would eventually encourage cognitive and institutional transformation of transactional relations between various segments of society. There should be concrete policy action to promote linkages between various levels of education in the country. There must also be efforts to promote peace and civic education to develop capacities for national reconciliation and long-term political sustainability. Postsecondary institutions should be given financial and material incentives to develop and implement curriculum frameworks that incorporate the value of experiential learning and the cultural knowledge of those participating in educational programs at all levels including adult and professional education. These efforts may also be geared at improving and making more relevant the accelerated learning programs that are currently being supported by international donor agencies.

The country through its democratic and governing institutions will need to fashion a new national identity that integrates the best traditions of its triple heritages: the African, Christian and Islamic heritages. Hence, we must now abandon and move away from the anachronistic renderings of the likes of Hilary Teage (1850s) and C.L.Simpson (1960s)—who because they did not understand the finer details and esoteric canons of the African heritage, failed to see the similarities between some aspects of our traditional cultural practices and the western tradition and modernity. In the tradition of the "rigorous" empiricism advocated by Hilary Teage, I would endeavor to prove this point by quoting him (see Burrowes, 1998, p.31):

> "Then pleading we shall be successful, and Liberia shall
> live before God and before the nations of the earth and
> become the focus where the rays of light emanating

from other lands shall meet. Hence they shall go out, diverging in every direction as they fly, piercing the darkness which for ages like a sable pall has mantled the generations of our fatherland until liberty and law and religion and love shall kindle a blaze of glory in this benighted land."

In the opinion of Hilary Teage, a blaze of glory was needed to ignite a benighted land beclouded by darkness into the age of liberty, law and religion. I would argue that what is required in current conditions, however, is the formation of a logical synthesis, which extols the practical value of personal and social transformations imbedded within the culture. This very tedious process ultimately involves specifying the determinants of our conscious actions that lead to social change and modernity.

This section has outlined some of the reasons for hope in the future and in the possibility of social change in Liberia after so many false starts. These reasons are imbedded in the realization that through critical consciousness we can energize the process of structural and institutional change. I have alluded to a deeper meaning of civilization that is situated and given form to by the nature of our consciousness. To this end I would argue that the search for civilization is essentially undergirded by the determinants of our motivations and critical consciousness. This search can be impeded or enhanced based on our ways of knowing, the quality of our insights, and modes of validation of our feelings and belief systems.

The section has also highlighted the conception of an indeterminate status or liminal condition as a delicate status in the process of personal transformation according to the esoteric rituals of the Poro societies in Liberia. Civil conflicts in Liberia have offered opportunities for exploitation of this ritual by warlords in their senseless assaults on innocent victims. What this shows is that callous individuals in their quest to subjugate others, especially where discourse and freedom are inhibited, can exploit any human institution or forms of authority and power relations. The civil war in Liberia has also led to the arbitrary demystification of the power of the Poro and Sande as enduring cultural institutions. This is not a surprise as the war has also had tremendous effects on other historical institutions and challenged our commitment to a moral heritage as a nation. Thus, the challenge of post war development is to restore the influence of these institutions by building upon and refining those aspects that appeal to our rational instincts and sense of modernity, such as the need to change or improve the way we interpret the meaning of our experiences, so that we may become co-creators of our historical destiny as well as productive and civic members of society. This, in the final analysis, will lead to a notion of common destiny, a cultural synthesis, and a civilized nation at ease with itself.

Chapter summary

This has further reinforced the view that the way out of moral and political decay in Liberia lies in participatory dialogue and critical consciousness. The most important point that has been underscored in the chapter is that a tradition of discipline, dialogue and personal transformation already exist within Liberian culture. These traditions and ethical norms are credible and authentic sources. These humanistic traditions composed of what I would regard as positive historical tendencies, which the nation cannot do without especially in times of great national stress. What is needed, therefore, and in fact what constitutes the greatest challenge for Liberian scholars and all those with interest in Liberian affairs is to find means and operative mechanisms by which these positive tendencies can be integrated within a broader and overarching framework of social practice and institutional action. The chapter reflected on the choice between barbarism and civilization and offered an operational definition of civilization within the context of social progress. Based on a more uplifting and humanistic definition of civilization, I have concluded that the nation must opt for civilization as a means of enhancing personal and social transformation.

The chapter has also specified instances of perspective transformation to demonstrate that there are some similarities at the functional level, between it and personal transformation occasioned by the Poro rite of passage. I have also concluded that critical consciousness as an instrumental objective in organizational processes in Liberia is undergirded by assumptions, which depart from a theory of motivation that is concerned with deciphering the meaning of an action. Finally, the chapter concluded that the way ahead for Liberia consists in instituting practices and frameworks in both formal and informal learning and educational processes that underscore the need to improve the way we as a nation and as adults in particular, interpret the meaning of our individual and collective experiences, so that we may become better and improved actors on the historical stage.

Chapter 6

Summary and Conclusion

"A populace that acquired the habit of discussion would keep the democratic spirit alive by fostering a continuous critical questioning of the directives and justifications of political leaders."

—Brookfield, 2001—

This book is about looking and going ahead, while not trying to repeat the mistakes of the past. In this book I have attempted to elaborate a framework for social progress, national dignity and modernity. This book is also about learning from our experiences so that we may take further action to recreate our lives in contemporary cultural and institutional arrangements. The idea of learning from our experiences through rational discourse and critical reflection is an amazing concept. I would declare in all honesty, that in order to do that, old patterns of interactions and structuring discourse must be transformed. This must be done to cope with new realities and new challenges within the context of our strivings for individual and collective empowerment.

We must seek to create the enabling social, economic and political environment within which power free communication and social democracy will flourish. This is my central message. But I am aware that this can only be done by seeking new avenues for social existence and dialogic patterns of interaction and legitimacy within the framework of the state and civil society. There is no doubt that the general elections to be held next October will have lasting impact and far reaching effects with regards to the structuring of new interactions in the social and institutional realms. For, the failures or successes of those elections will determine to a greater extent what path of development Liberia follows. It may make or break the quest for stability and social transformation in a society that disparately seeks them. Is this enough to remand us that the stakes could never be higher?

I should mention that this book has also been about the fostering of transformational learning in a historical and cultural context where it is most needed. And this is the socio-cultural and institutional milieu of Liberian society. The state of our society and body politic demands new forms of consciousness, institutional paradigms and cultural predispositions and practices. The book has also been geared toward laying some foundations regarding how education should be established and new platforms for institutional dialogues formed to aid the transformation process in the Liberian society. At the core of new thinking, perspectives and new institutional dialogues and arrangements in society, must be the predominance of power and dominance free communication. It is important to sound this again and again, so that its vital importance becomes crystal clear. A culture of dominance free communication is the bedrock of an open and just society. It is also presumably the most optimum medium of ensuring that everyone including market women and farmers in the remotest villages has an opportunity to be heard. It is a must that everyone be heard in the social system and our patterns of engagement with the political, cultural and economic worlds.

Everyone must be heard and must be allowed to inform a new covenant for peace, mutual respect, dignity, and sustained patterns of self-governance in the new post-conflict situation. The most important challenge, which I hope has resonated throughout this book is that we must oblige ourselves to devise mechanisms through our modern educational and cultural system by which this noble method can become embedded in our thinking processes and enduring constitutional and social practices. These practices will involved constantly learning from our collective and individual experiences as adults and conscious historical actors with the view of improving our interpretive stances and folk methods of problem solving.

The various chapters in this book have contributed in various ways to elucidating the theme and historical and intellectual project of transformation. Liberia requires deep-seated changes at the institutional, but even more importantly, at the cultural, cognitive and epistemic levels. In chapter one, I described the educational system in Liberia in terms of its basic structural features and constituent elements. I further alluded to the evolution of this system, which can be traced to the formative years of nationhood in the 19th century. However, it has been suggested that the education system in Liberia has consistently failed to tackle the problems of underachievement and to adopt appropriate strategies that would harness lifelong and independent learning, as a basis for the learning society.

This suggestion derives from an appreciation of the educational challenges facing the nation as outlined in the introductory chapter. The proof of educational failure has been demonstrated by various performance indicators such as the fact that after 150 years of formal education, the country still ranks among the least literate of the English-Speaking African countries. The country also has an education system that is incapable of coping with other most demanding and visible challenges of national reconstruction. Our present system is also incapable of harnessing and, indeed, coping with the new forms of consciousness and cultural practices critical to the creation of a new social order.

The fact that Liberia is the least literate of the English-Speaking countries in Africa with an average literacy rate of 30 percent and an annual growth rate of primary enrollment of 2.6 percent is significant. It has led to the recognition that our system of education has failed to meet its historic demands. This is why I have argued in the introductory chapter that changing learning outcomes and improving the institutional capacity for educational development, would require the reorientation of educational policies. Transformation in the structure and organization of learning will also require dialogic learning processes, and incorporation of the finest traditions of progressivism and criticism in education and democratic theory.

The need for educational reforms and the transformation of authority and institutional processes are justified by the challenges of globalization and rapid technological change in the 21st century. No nation can cope with these changes with such outdated intervention approaches and systems that we have. This is while I would argue that the inspiration for this work arose primarily out of the appreciation of the potential of adult education to make a material and tangible contribution to fostering democratic governance and participatory discourse in galvanizing for social action in civil society. The state and its machinery must also become comfortable with a change process so that such process cannot be inhabited. I hope readers were able to discern this important fact. For, in effect, elucidating this theme has been one of the central operational objectives, which this book hopes to accomplish as well.

In chapter one, I further cited a variety of sources, including primary and secondary sources. Such sources included, for example, articles from the Adult Education Quarterly—a major journal for the publication of cutting edge knowledge in the field of adult education, the Journal of Lifelong Learning, and various Jossey-Bass publications (books and handbooks) in the field of adult education etc. Impressions from classroom based participation-observation research and extensive interviews with Liberian professionals, policy makers, educational workers, students and teachers formed a part of this study.

Their views regarding education, critical reflection and cognitive and social change have been reflected throughout this book. The research questions which have been stipulated at the end of chapter two derived from an appreciation of the existing literature on transformational learning theory, and the need to apply this theory to the case of Liberia. The research questions also reflect a desire to identify fundamental issues and problems at the core of the quest to remake society so that it becomes a model haven of freedom and economic prosperity and an epicenter for peace and regional stability and cooperation.

Several methodological premises were outlined in chapter one. I stated that I would principally relied on the interpretive research paradigm, which is consistent with the epistemology of social constructivism. The interpretive tradition in social theory has been developed over the years by theorists such as Husserl, Heidegger, Gadamer, Schutz, Garfinkel etc. This account of scientific method contests sense of experience as posited by the positivist conception of the human sciences. The central tendency in social constructivism is the context dependence of all historical and social phenomena. This suggests that all social realities occur in a particular context and such context should be taken into account in the construction of meaning and a transformative praxis.

Readers may note that I have conducted a comprehensive review of those aspects of the literature related to the development of transformational learning theory since the late 1970s. The chapter began by emphasizing the critical role that Jack Mezirow's ideas on adult learning and education have played in advancing the theory and practice of transformative learning. Transformation theory enables us to deconstruct the categories of social reality at the most foundational levels. What this proposition suggests is that the process of transformation is the deconstructing of socially constructed experience, acting upon said experience, and finally reconstructing it (Merriam and Caffarella, 1993). I located transformation theory within the modern constructivist tradition of education. Following that, I then proceeded to discuss the main outlines of socio-constructivist theories.

I have also reviewed other pertinent theories of adult learning including theories of motivation, participation and self-determination. I considered various lines of research on the motives and causes of participation, including Miller's deterministic social class theory of participation. It was concluded that Miller's theory was built upon Maslow's needs hierarchy approach and the force field analysis of Lewin. I reviewed the self-determination theory of Deci and his collaborators. I would conclude that the issue of the vital role of social context featured prominently in the self-determination theory of these authors. The issue of the context dependence of our understanding of social phenomena also featured prominently in my understanding of transformation theory and democratic change.

I have further reviewed the works of cognitive theorists, which have focused and thrown light on the nature of cognitive and learning styles in traditional societies. I traced the research findings since the 1960s up to present, in order to establish some background in terms of elucidating the dynamics of social cognition in dual societies such as Liberia. It was posited that the nature of cognition in dual societies justifies the importance of experiential learning in meeting the fundamental aspirations for individual and social transformation. It was also emphasized in this chapter that the main strengths of experiential learning are intrinsic motivation and the development of practice through self-reflective learning.

My discussion has recognized the presumption that the ideal conditions of discourse are an important standard against which we measure the necessary and sufficient conditions for personal and social transformation. These ideal conditions are the same in Liberia as they are in other societies. I have argued in this book that it is self-evident that there is no empirical evidence to support a claim that the ideal conditions of discourse have ever existed nor do they exist at present in Liberian society. The available evidence as presented in this book in terms of the history of educational development in Liberia, and the nature of an overbearing state, affirmed the thesis that society must strive toward creating better conditions through constitutional and institutional arrangements for rational discourse and perspective transformation.

I view the creation of the learning society as an ideal not divorce from meeting the most basic challenges of governance and economic modernization. In Liberia the learning society can be achieved within the domains of communicative action and other spheres of interactions within the society. The formation of a national consensus on creating a future where civil society and appropriate democratic interest groups and institutions will assume a prominent role in national affairs and various forms of socio-economic transactions is situated at the core of one's conception of a learning society. I am of the opinion that the underlying structural features of this society will facilitate learning at all stages of the life circle and make it institutionalized as a universal phenomenon.

Chapter three of this book discussed the implications and imperatives of national reconstruction in Liberia. The chapter reaffirmed the need for national reconstruction in Liberia following many years of neglect and civil war in the country. The chapter reflected the economic and social costs of the civil war as well as the accentuation of crisis in the education system. The chapter called for grass roots participation in national decision-making on the basis of rational discourse and the need to foster collective social action for institutional change. The epigraph to chapter two encapsulates this message more eloquently—— that one's individual well-being and critical struggles are social in nature, and therefore, require mutually agreed upon strategies for change. Chapter four underscored the importance of fostering democratic dialogue as an instrument of engendering self-determination in civil society. Meanwhile, I sought to present a hypothetical example of ideal discourse in chapter five, where every participant in dialogue had an equal opportunity to participate in order to arrive at a tentative consensual best judgment, regarding what is and what ought to be, in the reconstitution of order in a society at drift.

The introduction to this work and the various chapters (from one to six) have all emphasized in one form or the other, that the principal emancipatory task of adult education and education in general, can be achieved by transformative modes of education and learning through the nurturing of countervailing tendencies in civil society and other democratic structures. It is suggested that these countervailing tendencies to restrict the influence of the state can be built through dialogic learning processes and other means of collaboration in the public sphere. Self-help projects and voluntary associations were name as prime examples of the social forces whose engagement in dialogue and democratic practices will lead to the re-creation of the lives of individuals in the space provided by a democratic civil society and state system.

Recommendations for policy development and change

This book has essentially examined the possibilities and modalities for fostering perspective transformation and social action in the Liberian society. In this section I will seek to reaffirm the various policy implications, which have come into focus in the last five chapters. It is significant to emphasize the point that institutional growth and participatory democracy are impossible in Liberia without deliberate public action through the formulation and implementation of appropriate policies to aid the growth process.

In the past there may have been policies to improve the atmosphere for free and unfettered access to national decision-making, but such policies have fell far short of expectations. There was the national unification and integration policy to increased participation in national affairs by ordinary citizens in the immediate postwar period under President William V.S. Tubman, for example. But what the discussion in this book has demonstrated is that when institutional power gets transform into personal power, the potential for perennial civil crisis and institutional decay increases exponentially. Thus, the prolonged crisis of national leadership and its related impact on the development potential of the Liberian nation is an ample testimony to the above assertion. What we need in Liberia above all are encumbered individuals who are in need of society.

For the thinking of encumbered individuals are formed by their multiple connections to society in terms of their social setting, family ties and the culture in which they are reared. A corollary of the encumbered individual is Boudieus' concept of habitus. Habitus is a sociological category referring to the phenomenon of the individual internalizing aspects of his or her culture. Indeed, an individual habitus is a vital link in mediating the impact of social structures, expectations, and external circumstances on individual action and behavior (Candy,1991,p.310).

What this amounts to is that the role of context is indispensable to understanding the underlying motivations of adults in society. Context can lead to an encumbered or unencumbered individual or individuals with all the sociological and political implications that that entails. In light of the discussions above, I would like to give some considerations to overriding policy issues, which invariably undergird the process of transformation, the formation of encumbered individuals and social empowerment.

These policy issues include for example, the adoption of a core curriculum that speaks to local conditions and cultural patterns. The function of a core curriculum that reflects national character is to ensure a humane approach to teaching and learning. Apart from transferring basic and higher order thinking and analytical skills, a core curriculum also validates the importance of the collective cultural capital of a nation. This cultural capital must be passed on from generation to generation through the process of socialization, which takes place in schools and other places of learning. These assertions prove the importance of a core curriculum as a foundation for fostering emancipatory learning and education in formal and informal learning settings in Liberia.

Another area to consider for improvement would be the national examinations. The national examinations must be further developed to serve as a guidepost for examining crucial educational variables and performance indicators, such as teacher quality, administrative competence, curriculum and instructional formats, motivational structures at schools etc. There should also be concrete policy action to promote linkages between various levels of education in the country. There must also be efforts to promote peace education to develop capacities for national reconciliation and political sustainability.

Postsecondary institutions and other levels of education should be given financial and material incentives so that they may develop and implement curriculum frameworks that incorporate the value of experiential learning and the cultural knowledge of those participating in educational programs at all levels, including adult and professional training. This study has shown that learning through critical reflection and dialogic approaches are primary determinants of administrative, communicative, and cultural competence. This suggests that the Liberian society should mobilize the forces of civil society to aid and facilitate this process, which is essentially a process of learning and taking corrective action.

The Liberian state should take policy action to improve the financial management of higher educational institutions. Giving money to schools and colleges is not sufficient; there must be proper accountability structures to ensure fiscal rectitude and prudence. Action must also be taken to improve public relations and to encourage the widespread use of information technologies in preparation for the establishment of the learning society. The central government should further support non-governmental and voluntary associations to launch study circles in urban and rural areas to improve civic consciousness and associational life in the society.

Recommendations for future research

These recommendations for future research in the field of transformational learning derived from a review of the related literature in chapter one of this book. It also derived from my understanding of empirical cases of perspective transformation. The recommendations also essentially derived from the numerous discussions I have hosted with friends and professional colleagues who have studied personal transformations from spiritual and deeply emotional perspectives. The first recommendation to be made here is that there should be further research to deepen our understanding of primary cultural differences in terms of the relationship between the modern and traditional sectors in dual societies.

Modern comparative educational research might provide clues to problems such as retention, academic underachievement and the lack of a permeable structure for the development of professional expertise. The analysis in this book shows that studies of institutional transformations and decline must constitute new lines of research in the development of transformation theory. What this book has demonstrated is that there is a dialectical link between perspective transformation and how one perceives the structure of authority relations as manifested in patterns of institutional development. This observation has been made in the literature on transformation theory (see Mezirow, 1990,1996, 2000). What have not been done sufficiently it seems, are concrete efforts to apply transformation theory to the social and institutional analysis of specific countries. The study of transformation should be about individuals as much as they should be about how institutions and communities can transform themselves to utilize the full range of innate and learned human capabilities and expertise. There is a void in this regard throughout the literature, and I hope this book has made a modest effort to fill this void.

Meaning perspectives and schemes have been significantly defined as being as much a function of cognitive and affective processes, as they reflect our individual and collective human actions to impose meanings on our daily experiences. We create our historical norms, institutional arrangements and value systems on the basis of these meaning perspectives and structures (Mezirow, 1985, 1989). Development in adulthood primarily "involves movement toward more developmentally advanced meaning structures." (Mezirow 1995, p. 51) Subsequently, the actions and predispositions of significant actors in political history, such as leaders, can also be explained in terms of the formation of meaning structures. What these presuppositions suggest is that in explaining the fundamental causes of state and institutional failures, social scientific methodologies must emphasize an approach that illuminates the biographical and contextual circumstances of significant actors in political and social history, such as national leaders.

This view essentially calls for research approaches, which might lead to more holistic methodologies, incorporating structuralist (sociological) approaches with constructive developmental theories and findings of empirical research (see chapter one). Given this acknowledgement, I wish therefore, to propose further research on the basis of interdisciplinary approaches to yield new understandings in terms of the historic mission of adult education, which is to foster individual and social emancipation. I wish also that this study has broken new grounds and made a modest contribution to the debate on transformative learning as a generic theory of adult education. The most essential point I hope I have succeeded in making in this book is the fact that the art of nation building is ultimately a learning process, whereby there are moments of crises, insights, self-teaching and critical assessments of assumptions. The rhythm of this process is often connected to, and reflective of, the general rhythm of human and social history. We have observed this historical dynamic and its ups and downs since the beginning of times. In this particular connection today is no different from yesterday, nor will it be substantially different from tomorrow. In Liberia the old ways of doing things have failed. Therefore, what we need most are new perspectives to serve as guideposts for success as we struggle to change the flavor of our national discourse in the 21st century.

[Appendix 1]

Interview protocol
Instructor evaluation form

Designed by: Tarnue Johnson

<u>Students:</u> Please be honest in answering these questions. Information disclosed here would remain confidential. You do not need to write your name on this form.

Instructor's Name: Date:

Class:

Please rate the instructor based on the following scale.

1 = Poor   2 = Needs Improvement   3 = Average
4 = Good   5 = Excellent

1. The instructor was prepared and knowledgeable about the course content: -------
2. The instructor was enthusiastic about the subjects-------
3. The instructor answered all of my questions and was easy to understand: -------
4. Overall experience with the instructor------
5. The instructor's service was worthwhile to me: -----
6. What was the most important lesson you learn from the instructor--
   ----

   ----

7. How has your understanding of the requirements for college improved? ---
   ----

   ----

8. After this I am more enthusiastic about going to college:
   Yes   No   (Circle one)

Please write any additional comments or suggestions: ------------------
----

[Appendix 2]

The process of perspective transformation

Designed by: Tarnue Johnson

Key Informants/Participants: --

Learning activities that incorporate the use of critical thinking may serve as boosters or precursors for perspective transformation—a fundamental change in the way we interpret the meaning of our experience and the world around us.

The ten stages of perspective transformation as first described by Jack Mezirow (2002):
Stage 1: a disorienting dilemma;
Stage 2: self-examination;
Stage 3: a critical assessment of socio-cultural/epistemic/psychic assumptions;

Stage 4: relating one's discontent to similar experiences of others (i.e. discovering the common ground);
Stage 5: exploring new ways of acting;
Stage 6: building competence and confidence in new roles;
Stage7: planning a course of action;
Stage 8: acquiring knowledge and skills for implementing one's plan;
Stage 9: provisional efforts to try new roles; and
Stage 10: a reintegration into society on the basis of the conditions dictated by the new perspective.

Questions regarding socio-cultural assumptions [race, education and self-esteem]. These questions relate to stage three of the process of transformation.

1) What stereotypes do you have about other races?------------------
----
----

2) Has there been any significant change in your stereotypes of late?--
----

3) If so, what particular incident(s) triggered this change?----------
----

----

4) What is the meaning of education to you?-------------------------
----

----

5) Where do you get this meaning of education from----parents, society at large, movies, friends, school or other?------------------
----

----

6) What is the most challenging academic task for you?--------------
----

----

7) Why is this so?--

----

8) How is completing this program going to help you in your
   personal and professional life?---

----

9) What is your self-esteem level at this stage? High, low, not so
   high?---

----

10) Is your self-esteem level at present in any way related to your
    failures or successes in life? How?--

Note: The facilitator should first describe the 10 stages of perspective transformation as outlined above, and explain their relationship to personal development before handing out this questionnaire to clients. In order to gain more insight into how to assist clients to achieve personal transformation, especially in regard to their prior assumptions about the value of postsecondary education or education in general, the facilitator should give additional writing assignments whereby clients would amply reflect on their prior assumptions, views, feelings and mindsets. These historical and educational autobiographies can be a vital too in elucidating the meaning and processes of change.

[Appendix 3]

Interview protocol
The process of perspective transformation

Designed by: Tarnue Johnson

Key Informants: --------------------------
----

1) How have you critically reflected on your experience of taking part in the first section of the college preparatory program?-----
----

----

2) In what ways have your previous assumptions about going to college stopped you from coming to this type of college preparatory program?---
----
----

3) How did coming to this program change your mind about going to college? --

----

----

4) How has this program helped you in becoming an independent student? ---

----

5) How have your views about life in general changed after your first four weeks in this program? --

----

----

6) Has coming to this program affected your personality in any way? If so, how? --

----

[Appendix 4]

Interview protocol
Social and educational change in Liberia

Designed by: Tarnue Johnson

Key Informant: ------------------------
----

1) How would you describe the greatest challenge facing Liberia today? ---
   ----

2) What is the greatest educational challenge in the country? ------
   ----
   ----

3) How can we reform primary education? -----------------------------
   ----
   ----

4) How about secondary education? -------------------------------------
----
----

5) How can we reform postsecondary education? --------------------
----
----

6) I have learnt that the entire school system has broken even in
places like Firestone that used to have better conditions in pre
civil war years; how can we fix it? ---------------------------------
----

----

7) Some people have argued that we should give more powers to
parents, teachers, school administrators and community leaders
in terms of how they decide to educate their children; what are
your views regarding these sentiments? How would you justify
those views? ---

----

8) In what ways have relationships and family structures being
affected by the war? ---
----

9) Do you think the situation in Liberia will ever get better, if so,
why and how? --

----

10) What are your views on the issuing elections in October 2005?

----

11) What role do you think dialogue and peaceful negotiations play
in settling conflicts and differences between the various ethic
groups in Liberia? ---
----

12) What in your view should be the role of Liberians in the Diaspora
in the reconstruction of their country? ----------------------------
----

----

13) What are you views on constitutional change in Liberia? ---------
----

14) What are your views on presidential power in Liberia? ------------
----
----

15) What role do you think some politicians and warlords have played in igniting ethnic tensions in Liberia? ----------------------
----
----

16) What are your views on the need for a war crimes tribunal in Liberia? --
----

----

17) What should become of the ex-president Charles Taylor in your opinion? --
----

----

18) What are the most important changes that have taken place in your views toward Liberia and Liberians since you left? -----------
----

----

19) What kind of person do you think should become the next president of Liberia? --
----

[Appendix 5]
Interview protocol
Personal transformation

Key Informant: -------------------------------------

----

1) What has been the single most significant event in your life since the war in Liberia? ---
   ----

----

2) In what ways has the war in Liberia affected your views about human society? --
----

[Appendix 6]

An interview schedule for the investigation of current issues facing the Liberian educational system at the classroom and policy levels.

Designed by: Tarnue Johnson

Key Informant: ------------------------------

Questions:

1) How many years were you involved with the educational system in Liberia? --- --- --- ---------------

2) In what capacity(s) were you involved with the educational system in Liberia? --- ---

3) If you were a teacher, what subject(s) did you teach and at what level of the educational system? --

4) Did you think you accomplished anything worthwhile in terms of helping students learned? --

5) How would you describe your experience as a teacher/lecturer compared to your school days in Liberia? What things have changed? And what remained the same? ----------------------------

6) What were your most memorable impressions in terms of where we are as a nation in educating future leaders today? -------------

7) In what ways are the difficult economic and security situation in Liberia affecting the school system? ------------------------------------

8) Are there any meaningful efforts on the part of policy makers to rebuild the educational system after so much destruction during the years? --

9) In what ways do you think our school system today can be improved? --

10) What can we do precisely to improve teacher quality? How can we upgrade the content of the school curriculum? ------------------

11) In what ways do the lack of proper remuneration for teachers and other education workers affect the quality of educational outcomes? --

12) What are your views on the rapid growth of tertiary colleges in Monrovia? Are there any meaningful ways such efforts on the part of private individuals and organizations can be properly regulated? --
----

13) What is the average qualification(s) of teachers/lecturers teaching in these new colleges in and around Monrovia? ------
----

----

14) How do these private colleges generally get their funding to operate? ---
----

References

America's Defense Monitor (1998) ADM's Glenn Baker interviews Conmany Wesseh, Center for Democratic Empowerment, Liberia, for "Light Weapons, Heavy Casualties" Available at: http://www.cdi.org/adm/1216/Wesseh.html.

Ajzen, I. (1998) Attitudes, personality and behavior. Chicago, Illinois: The Dorsey Press.

Atlas, J. (1989) Philosophy without ambiguity. Oxford: Oxford University Press.

Appiah, K.. A. (1992) In my father's house: Africa in the philosophy of Culture: New York: Oxford University Press.

Austin, J.(1960) How to do things with words. Oxford: Oxford University Press

Argyris, C. and Schon, D. (1978) Organizational Learning: A theory of action perspective. Reading, Mass: Addison Wesley.

Bach, K and Harnish,R. (1979) "Linguistic communication: A schema for speech acts", in Pragmatics: A reader, ed. Steven Davis. New York: Oxford University Press

Bach, K. (1987) Thought and Reference. Oxford: Oxford University Press.

Bach, K. (1994) Conversational implicature. Mind and Language, 9,124-162

Bach, K. and Harnish, R. (1992) How performatives really work: A reply to Searle. Linguistics and Philosophy, 15, 93-110

Bach, K. (2003) The Semantics-Pragmatics Distinction: What it is and why it matters. Retrieved in 2003 and available at: http:www//online. sfsu.edu/

Bellman, B. L. (1984) The Language of Secrecy: Symbols and Metaphors in Poro ritual. New Jersey: Rutgers University Press.

Bernard, R. (1995) Research methods in anthropology: Qualitative and quantitative approaches. New York: Altamira Press

Berry, W. (1976) Human ecology and cognitive style. New York: Wiley and sons

Berstein, R. (Ed) (1985) Habermas and modernity. Cambridge Mass: MIT Press

Berverly, J.(1993) Teacher as researcher. ERIC Clearing on teacher education Washington DC. ERIC DIGEST

Blinder, A. (1986) "Keynes after Lucas." Eastern Economic Journal (July-September): 209-216.

Bohm, D. and Associates (1991) Dialogue: A Proposal. Retrieved in 2003 and available at http://www.infed.org.

Brookfield, S. (1985) A critical definition of adult education, Adult Education Quarterly, 36, 1, 44-49.

Brookfield, S. (1986) Understanding and facilitating adult learning. San Francisco: Jossey Bass.

Brookfield, S. (1987) Developing critical thinkers. San Francisco: Jossey-Bass.

Brookfield, S. (1988) Developing critically reflective practitioners: A rationale for training educators of adults in Brookfield, S. (Ed) Training educators of adults: Theory and practice of adult education in North America, London: Routledge.

Brookfield, S. (1993) Understanding consulting as an adult education process in Zachary, L. and Vernon, S. (Eds) The adult educator as consultant, No. 58, summer, San Francisco: Jossey- Bass.

Brookfield, S. (1995) Adult learning: An overview. In A. Tuinjmn (Ed) International Encyclopedia of education. Oxford: Pergamon Press.

Brookfield, S. (2000) The concept of critically reflective practice. Wilson A. and Hayes, E.(Eds) The concept of critically reflective practice. San Francisco: Jossey-Bass.

Brookfield, S. (2000) Tranformative learning as ideology critique. In J. Mezirow and Associates (Eds) Learning as transformation: Critical perspective on a theory in progress. San Francisco: Jossey-Bass

Brookfield, S. (2001) A political analysis of discussion groups: Can the circle be broken? In Cervero, R. M., and Wilson, A. L. (Eds) Power in practice: Adult education and the struggle for knowledge and power in society. San Francisco: Jossey –Bass.

Brookfield, S. (forthcoming) Adult cognition as a dimension of lifelong learning. To be publish in lifelong learning: Education across the lifespan. (Eds) Field, J. and Leicester, M. Philadelphia: Falmer Press.

Burbles, N. C. (1993) Rethinking Rationality: On learning to be reasonable. Retrieved in 2003 and available at http://www.edu.uiuc.edu.

Burrowes, C. P. (1989) The Americo-Liberian ruling class and other myths: A critique of scholarship on Liberia. Occasional Paper No. 3. Institute for African-American Affairs, Department of African-American Studies, Temple University, Philadelphia, Pennsylvania.

Burrowes, C. P. (1998) Cornerstones of a Nation. Lectures to the Liberian Lyceum by Joseph Jenkins Roberts, John Naustedlau Lewis and Hilary Teage in 1845 with an introduction by Carl Patrick Burrowes, Liberian Research and Information Project.

Candy, P. C. (1991) Self-direction for lifelong learning. San Francisco: Jossey Bass Publishers.

Carr-Hill, R. (Ed) Adult literacy programs in Uganda. The World Bank, Washington: First Printing.

Cassell, A. (1983) History of Liberia: A time line. New York: Macmillan Publishers.

Clark, C. M. and Wilson, A. R. (1991) Context and rationality in Mezirow's theory of transformational learning. Adult Education Quarterly, 41, 2, 75-91.

Colclough, C. (1990) Raising additional resources for education in developing countries: Are graduate payroll taxes superior to student loans? International Journal of Educational Development, 24, 169-180.

Colclough, C. (Ed) (1997) Marketing education and health in developing countries, Oxford: Clarendon Press

Cole, M. and Bruner, J. (1971) Cultural differences and influences about psychological processes. American Psychologist, 26, 867-876.

Collard, S. and Law, M. (1989) The limits of perspective transformation: A critical review of Mezirow's theory. Adult Education Quarterly, 39, 99-107.

Collins, M. (1991) Adult education as vocation: A critical role for the adult educator. Routledge: London

Collins, R.(1986) Max Weber: A Skeleton Key. Masters of social theory volume 3. Sage Publications, London.

Constitution of the Republic of Liberia. Available at http://www. republicofliberia/

Cornia, A. and Associates (1987) Adjustment with a human face: Protecting the vulnerable and promoting growth, Oxford: Clarendon House.

Courtney, S. (1991) Why adults learn: Toward a theory of participation in adult education. New York: Routledge.

Cranton, P. (1994) Understanding and promoting transformative learning: A guide for educators of adults. San Francisco: Jossey-Bass.

Cross, P. (1981) Adults as learners: Increasing participation and facilitating learning. San Francisco: Jossey-Bass.

Daniel, K. and Daniel, H. (1990) Education as a social agent: One university's answer to a multiethnic graduate adult population. In Cassara, B. (Ed) Adult education in a multicultural society. London: Roudledge.

Dahn, M. (2001) Technical education: One of the vehicles to settle Liberia's palaver. Presented to the Liberian community in Georgia, Atlanta. (Unpublished).

Darkenwald, G. and Merriam, S. (1982) Adult education: Foundations of practice. New York: Happer and Row Publishers.

Darkwa, O. and Mazibuko, F. (2000) Creating virtual learning communities in Africa: Challenges and prospects. Retrieved in 2004 and available at: http:www.firstmonday.dk/irrrus/irrus5.5/darkwa

Davidson, B.(1991) Africa in history: Themes and outlines. New York: Collier Books

Deci, E. (1971) Effects of externally mediated rewards on intrinsic motivation. Journal of Personality and Social Psychology, 18, 105-115.

Deci, E., Vallerand, R., and Ryan, R. (1991) Motivation and education: The self-determination perspective, Educational Psychologist, 26,325-346.

Diop, C. (1991) Civilization or barbarism: an authentic anthropology, Lawrence Hill Books, Presence Africaine, Paris

Dirkx, J. (2000) "Its time to change our minds: An introduction to transformative learning," Revision, 20,2.

Dunn, E. and Hosoe, S. (1985) Historical dictionary of Liberia. African historical dictionaries, series No. 38. New Jersey: Scarrecrow Press

Dunn, E. and Tarr, B. (1988) Liberia : A national polity in transition. New York: The Scarcecrow Press Inc.

Ellis, S. (1999) The mask of anarchy: The destruction of Liberia and the religious dimensions of the civil war, New York University Press, New York

Engels, F. (1946) Ludwig Feuerbach and the end of classical German philosophy, Progress Publishers, Moscow.

Ettling, D. (2003) The praxis of sustaining transformative change. Retrieved in 2003 and available at: TCRecord.Org. University of Columbia.

Fanon, F. (1963) The watched of the earth. New York: Grove Press.

Fanon, F. (1967) Black Skin, White Masks. New York: Grove Press Inc.

Fishbein, M., and Ajzen, I. (2003) Theory of reasoned action/ Theory of planned behavior. Retrieved in 2003 and available at: http://www.medusf.edu/~kmbrown?TBA_TPA.htm

Fleming, T. (2002) Habermas on civil society, lifeworld and system: Unearthing the social in transformation theory. TCRecord.Org, University of Columbia.

Foucault, M. (1961) Madness and Civilization: A history of insanity in the age of reason, translated from the French by Richard Howard, Travistock, London, 1967.

Frankel, M. (1964) Tribe and class in Monrovia. New York: Oxford University Press

Freepong, D. State formation and collapse in Liberia. Retrieved in 2004 and avialable at http://www.valthelsink.fi/

Fuller, B. (1989-1990) Eroding economy, declining school quality: The case of Malawi, IDS Bulletin, Vols. 20-21.

Gates, H. L. (1988) The Signifying Monkey: A theory of African-American literary criticism. Oxford. Oxford University Press.

Gaunnu, J. (1980) The inaugural address of the Presidents of Liberia: From Joseph Roberts to William R. Tolbert. New York: Exposition Press.

Garfinkel, J. (1967) Studies in ethnomethodology. New Jersey: Harper and Herter.

Garfinkel, J., and Sacks, H. (1970) On formal structures and practical actions. In J. C. Mickinney and E. A. Tiryakian (Eds) Theoretical sociology: Perspectives and development. New York: Appleton-Century- Crofts.

Garvey, M. (1935) Modern Man. Retrieved in 2004 and available at: http://www.boomshaka.com/garvey/modern.html

Geertz, C. (1973) The interpretation of culture. New York: Basic Books.
Gershoni, Y. (1985) Black Colonialism: The Americo-Liberian scramble for the hinterland. Westview Special Studies on Africa.

Giroux, H. A. (1995) Schooling as a form of cultural politics: Toward a pedagogy of and for difference. In Groux, H. A. and Mclaren (Eds) Critical pedagogy, the state, and the cultural struggle. New York: State University of New York Press.

Graham, S. (1997) Using attribution theory to understand social and academic motivation in African American Youth. Educational Psychologist, 32, 21-34.

Grootaert, C. (1994) Education, poverty, and structural change in Africa: Lessons from Cote D'Ivore, International Journal of Educational Development, 14, 2, 131-142.

Gustavsson, B. and Harung, H. (1994) Organizational learning based on transforming collective consciousness, available at http://www.fek.su.se/Home/gus/PAPERS/

Habermas, J. (1987) The idea of the theory of knowledge as social theory. Cambridge: Polity Press.

Haddad, M. (1990) Liberia's illusive dream of democracy. The Perspective, 4, 2, 8-10.

Hart, M. (1990) Critical theory and beyond: Further perspectives on emancipatory education, Adult Education Quarterly, 40, 125-138.

Hale-Benson, J. (9182) Black children: Their roots, culture, and learning styles. Baltimore: John Hopkins University Press.

Heany, T. (2000) Adult education for social change: From center stage to the wings and back again. Columbus, OH: ERIC Clearinghouse on Adult, Career, and Vocational Education.

Hinchliff, K.. (1989-1990) Economic austerity, structural adjustment and education: The case of Nigeria, IDS Bulletin, Vols. 20-21.

Hoffman, D. M. (1995) Models of self and culture in teaching and learning, Educational Foundations: Caddo Group Press.

Houle, C. O. (1961) The inquiring mind. Madison: University of Wisconsin Press.

Houle, C. O. (1980) Continuing learning in the professions. San Francisco: Jossey-Bass.

Horton, R. (1967) African traditional thought and western science. Africa, 37, 157-187.

Howard, K. W. (1989) A comprehensive expectancy motivation model: Implications for adult education and training, Adult Education Quarterly, 39, 199-210.

Husen and Postlethwaite (Eds) (1994) The International Enclypedia of Education. V0l. 1 and Vol. 3. London: Pergomon.

Imel, S. (1996) Distance education: Trends and issues alert. ERIC educational resources information center. Available at: http://www.erocacve.org/

Immel, S. (1999) How emancipatory is adult learning? ERIC Educational Resources Information Center. Myths and Realities. No. 6.

Inglis, T.(1997) Empowerment and emancipation. Adult Education Quarterly, 45, 3-17.

Inglis, T. (1998) A critical realist approach to emancipation: A response to Mezirow. Adult Education Quarterly, 49, 72-76.

Jarvis, P. (1987) Meaningful and meaningless experience: Towards an analysis of learning from life, Adult Education Quarterly, 37, 3, 164-172.

Jarvis P. (1987) Adult learning in the social context. New York: Croom Healm.

Jarves, P. (1995) Adult and continuing education: Theory and practice, London: Routledge

Jean, L. (1977) Cognitive consequences of traditional apprenticeship training in West Africa. Anthropology and Education Quarterly, 8, 177-180.

Jimenez, E. (1986) The public subsidization of education and health in developing countries: A review of equity and efficiency, The World Bank Research Observer, 6, 205-218.

Jimenez, E. (1991) The relative efficiency of private and public schools in developing countries, The World Bank Research Observer, 6, 313-329.

Johnson, C. (1987) Bitter Canaan: The story of the Negro Republic. Transaction Books, New Brunswick (USU)

Johnson, T. (2001) Empowerment education: A guide to curriculum reforms in Liberia. Available at http://www.theperspective.org/

Johnson, T. (2002) Educational leadership and other determinants of academic achievement in Liberia. Available at http://www.theperspective.org/

Johnson, T.(2002) New Perspectives on the Causes and Consequences of Institutional Decline in Liberia. Available at http://www.theperspective.org/

Johnson, T. (2002) The determinants of academic achievement in Liberia. Available at: http:www.theperspective.org/

Johnson, T. (2002) The role of education in strengthening civil society in Liberia: A new agenda for self-emancipation and social change. Available at: http://www.theperspective.org/

Johnson, T. (2003) Fostering transformative learning and social action in Liberia: New perspectives for the 21st century (An Extended Review), The African Symposium: A Journal of Educational Research on Africa, Vol.3, No.4,

Johnson, T. (2003) Liberia in crisis: The structure and underlying causes of a national failure. Available at http://www.theperspective.org/

Johnson, T., and Patrick, C. (2003) A symposium: On paradoxes, autocracy and the betrayal of a nation. Available at: http://www.theperspective.org/

Johnson, T.(2004)The beginning of our time. Available at: http://www.theperspective.org/

Jones, E. S. (2004) The need to decentralized governance in post-war Liberia. Available at: http://www.newdemocrat.org/30mayJonesdecentralised.html

Kamara, T. (2000) Diamonds, war and state collapse in Liberia and Sierra Leone. The Perspective, 4, 2, 4-8.

Kathleen, K. (1998) How adult learners change in higher education. Retrieved in 2003 and available at: http://www.edst.educ.ubc.ca/aerc/1998/98king.htm.

Kegan, R. (2000) A Constructive Developmental Approach to Transformation in Mezirow (ed) Learning as transformation: Critical perspectives on a theory in progress, San Francisco: Jossey-Bass.

Karnga, A. (1926) History of Liberia. Liverpool: D. H. Tyte.

Kasl, E. and Yorks, L. (2002) An extended epistemology for transformative learning theory and its application through collaborative inquiry. TCR Record.Org. Teachers College, Columbia University.

Keane, J. (1988) Democratic and civil society, London: Verso.

Kidd, R. (1973) How adults learn. New York: Association Press.

Knapp, P. (1994) One world-many worlds: Contemporary sociological theory. New York: Harper Collins

Knox, A. B. (1986) Helping adults learn. San Francisco: Jossey-Bass.

Kortian, G. (1980) Metacritique: The philosophical argument of Jumgen Habermas. Cambridge: Cambridge University Press.

Kurian, G. World education encyclopedia. New York: Facts on file publications.

Lashway, L. (1988) Can instructional leaders be facilitative leaders? ERIC DIGEST, No. 98.

Lewin, K. (1947) Frontiers in group dynamics: Concept, method and reality in social science. Human Rources, 1, 5-41.

Liebenow, G. (1969) Liberia: The evolution of priviledge. Ithaca: Cornell University Press

Lowenkopf, M. (1976) Politics in Liberia: The conservative road to development. California: Hoover Institute Press.

Lynch, H. R. (1978) Selected letters of Edward Wilmont Blyden, KTO Press, United States.

Makoba, W. The role of African's culture in Economic Development. Available at http://www.afrst.uiuc.edu/Makerere/

Maiese, Michelle (2004) The notion of fair distribution. Retrieved in 2004 and available at:
http: www.intractableconflict.org/m/distributive_justice.jsp

Maladies, Michael, Dialogue as conflict resolution. Retrieved in 2004 and available at: http:ww.sedos.org.English/amaladoss1.html

Maslow, A. H. (1954) Motivation and personality. New York: Harper and Row .

Mayson, D. and Sawyer, A. (1979) Labour in Liberia. Review of African Political Economy, 6, 3-15

McCombs, B. (1991) Motivation and lifelong learning. Educational Psychologist, 26, 117-127

McLaren, P. (1986) Schooling as a ritual performance: Towards a political economy of educational symbols and gestures. London: Routledge.

Merriam, S. B. (1987) Adult learning and theory building. Adult Education Quarterly, 37, 187-198.

Merriam, S. B. (1989) Contributions of qualitative research to adult education, Adult Education Quarterly,39,161-168.

Merriam, S. B., and Caffarella, R. S. (1999) Learning in adulthood: A comprehensive guide. San Francisco-Jossey Bass.

Mezirow, J. (1981) A critical theory of adult learning and education. Adult Education, 32, 3-24

Mezirow, J. (1985a) Concept and action in adult education. Adult Education Quarterly, 35,142-151.

Mezirow, J. (1985b) A critical theory of self-directed learning. S. Brookfield (ed) New directions in continuing education. No.25, San Francisco: Jossey Bass.

Mezirow, J. (1989) Transformation theory and social action: A response to Collard and Law, Adult Education Quarterly. 39, 3, 169-175.

Mezirow, J. (1991) Transformation Theory and Cultural Context: A reply to Clark and Wilson. Adult Education Quarterly. 41,3,188-192

Mezirow, J. (1995) Transformation theory and adult learning. M. Welton (Ed) In defense of the lifeworld: Critical perspectives on adult learning. San Francisco: Jossey Bass

Mezirow, J. (1998) On critical reflection. Adult Education Quarterly, 48,3, 185-198.

Mezirow, J. and Associates (2000) Learning as transformation: Critical perspectives on a theory in progress. San Francisco: Jossey-Bass.

Miller, H. L. (1967) Participation of adults in education: A force field analysis. Boston: Center for the study of liberal education for adults, Boston University.

Miller, T. D., and Ratner, R. K. (1998) The disparity between the actual and assumed power of self-interest, 74, 1, 53-62.

Mills, R. (1987) Substance abuse, drop out and delinquency prevention: An innovative approach. Maima: The Moello-homestead gardens public housing early intervention project.

Mishler, E. (1979) "Meaning in context: Is there any other kind?" Harvard Rducational Review, 49, 1-18.

Moran, M. (1990) Civilized Women: Gender and prestige in southeastern Liberia. Cornell University Press. Ithaca and London.

Nelson, T. (1982) The Holy Bible, New King James Version. Thomas Nelson Inc.

Ogbu, J. (1987) Variability in minority school performance: A problem in search of a solution. Anthropology and Education Quarterly, 18, 312-334.

Ogbu, J. (1992) Understanding cultural diversity and learning. Educational Researcher, 21-5-157.

Oliver, L. (1987) Study circles: Coming together for personal growth and social change. Washington: Seven Locks Press.

Parkin, F. (1982) Max Weber, Travistok Publications. London.

Patterson, H. (1973) Humanistic education. Columbus: Merill.

Perin, D. (2002) Academic-Occupational integration as a reform strategy for the community colleges: Classroom perspectives. TCRecord.Org. Teachers College, Columbia University.

Perry, R. C. (2002) Independent Media: Liberia's key to peace and reconciliation. Available at:
http://www.theperspective.org/perry_remark.html

Peskett, D.(2001) Citizenship and education. A critical discourse analysis of the current Labour Government's initial guidance to schools on the introduction of Citizenship education. A paper presented for the 51st Political Studies Association conference. April 10-12, 2001, Manchester, UK.

Pepper, S. (1970) World hypothesis: A study in evidence. Berkeley: University of California Press.

Peterson, B. and Neil, M. (1999) Alternative to standardized tests. Rethinking Schools, 13, 3. Available at:
http://www.rethinkingschools.org.

Pryor, B. (1990) Predicting and explaining intention to participate in continuing education: An application of the theory of reasoned action. Adult Education Quarterly, 40, 147-157.

Rachal, J. (2003) A Symposium. Adult Education Quarterly, 54,1,59-72

Ramirez, M. and Castenada, A. (1974) Cultural democracy, bicognitive development and education, New York: Academic Press.

Rapaport, E. (Ed) (1978) J. S. Mill on liberty. Indianapolis: Hackett Publishing.

Reno, W. (1995) The reinvention of an African state: Charles Taylor's Liberia, Third World Quarterly, 16, 111-112.

Rice, R. and Richlin, L. (1993) Broadening the concept of scholarship in the professions. In Curry, L. and Associates (Eds) Educating the professional: Responding to new expectations for competence and accountability. San Francisco: Jossey-Bass.

Rodgers, C. (1969) Freedom to lean: A view of what education might become. Coulumbus, Ohio: Merill.

Rodgers, C. (2000) Defining reflection: Another look at John Dewey and reflective thinking. TCRecord.Org. Teachers College. Columbia University.

Rose, A. (1968) Building an indigenous elementary social studies curriculum: A look at what's happening in Liberia, West Africa. Indiana University.

Rubenson, K. (1977) Participation in recurrent education: A research review. A paper presented at a meeting of national delegates on developments in recurrent education, Paris.

Rubenson, K. (1989) The sociology of adult education. In Merriam, S. B. and Cunningham, P. M. (Eds) Hanbook of adult and continuing education. San Francisco- Jossey-Bass.

Rutherford, P. (2000) Endless propaganda: The advertising of public goods. Toronto: University of Toronto Press.

Salomon, G. (1993) 'No distribution without individual's cognition: A dynamic interactional view' in G. Salomon(ed) Distributed cognitions-Psychological and educational considerations (pp111-138). Cambridge, Cambridge University Press.

Samoff, J. (1990) The politics of privatization in Tanzania, International Journal of Educational Development, 10, 1, 1-15.

Sandra, K. (2000) Lifelong learning. Myths and realities. No. 9, ERIC DIGEST NO:441180

Sawyer, A. (1988) Effective Immediately: Dictatorship in Liberia, 1980-1986: A Personal Perspective. The Netherlands. The African Center.

Sawyer, A. (1992) The emergence of autocracy in Liberia: Tragedy and challenge. ICS Press, San Francisco, California.

Sawyer, A. (2004) A letter to the Chairman of the National Transitional Government of Liberia. Available at: http://wwwtheperspective.org/

Scanlan, C. and Darkenwald, G. (1984) Identifying deterrents to participation in continuing education, Adult Education Quarterly, 34, 155-166.

Schon, D. (1983) The reflective practitioner: How professionals think in action. New York: Basic Books.

Schunk, H. (1991) Self-efficacy and academic motivation. Educational Perspective, 26, 207-231.

Scribner, S. and Cole, M. (1981) The Psychology of Literacy. Cambridge. Mass: Harvard University Press.

Seibel, H. and Massing, A. (1974) Traditional organizations and economic development: Studies of indigenous cooperatives in Liberia: New York: Prager Publishers.

Seyon, P. (1997) Rebuiding the University of Liberia in the midst of war. International Higher Education, Boston College. Avialable at: http//www.bc.edu/

Shade, B. (Ed) (1989) Culture, style and the educative process. Springfield: Charles C. Thomas.

Shick, T. (1977) Behold the Promised Land: A History of Afro-American settler society in 19th century Liberia. Baltimore: the John Hopkins University Press.

Shor, I. (1992) Empowering education: Critical teaching for social change. Chicago: University of Chicago Press.

Simpson, G. (1998) Contested notions of reconciliation: The changing nature of violence on post-apartheid Africa. Available at: http://www.csvr.org.za/articles/

Sirleaf, E. J. (1999) Liberia: A framework for change and renewal. Presented at the conference on the Liberian economy. Unity Conference Center. Available at: http://www.theperspective.org

Somah, S. (2004) Charting a new direction for a traumatized Liberia. Available at: http://www.theperspective.org/

Soros, G. (1998) The crisis of global capitalism: Open society endangered. Little, Brown and Company.

Stein, D. (1998) Situated learning in adult education. ERIC Educational Information Center. ERIC DIGEST NO. 195.

Sudiata, I.K. (1990) Black Scandal: America and the Liberian labor crisis, 1929-1936, Philadelphia: Institute for the study of human issues.

Sudman, S. (1976) Applied Sampling. New York: Academic Press.

Susan, I. (1996) Distance education: Trends and issues alert. Available at: http://www.ericacve.org/

Szczelkun, S. (1999) Summary of the theory of communicative action. Retrieved on 2004 and available at http://www.csudh.edu/

Talcott, P. (1951) The social system. New York: Free Press.

Talcott, P. (1967) Sociological theory and modern society. New York: Free Press.

Taylor, E. (1997) "Building upon the theoretical debate: A critical review of the empirical studies Mezirow's transformative learning theory. Adult Education Quarterly, 48, 351-375.

Taylor, E. (1998) "The theory and practice of transformative learning: A critical review." Columbus Ohio: ERIC clearing house on Adult, Career, and Vocational Education (Information series, No. 374).

Taylor, E. (2000) Analyzing research on transformative learning theory. In J. Mezirow and Associates (Eds) San Francisco; Jossey Bass.

Tennant, M. and Pogson, P. (1995) Learning and change in the adult years: A developing perspective. San Francisco-Jossey Bass.

The Columbia Encyclopedia (2001) New York: Columbia University Press.

The constitution of the commonwealth of Liberia: Adopted by the Board of Directors of the American Colonization Society, January 5, 1839. Retrieved in 2003 and available at: http://wwwtoptags.com/

The Lawyers committee (1986) Liberia: A promised betrayed. New York: The lawyers committee for human rights.

The Perspective (2003) A joint statement issued by representatives of political parties. Available at http://www.theperspective.org/

Tiepoh, G.(2004) Liberians: Caught in political dilemma and new global realities. Retrieved in 2004 and available at: http://www.theperspective.org/

Tokpa, H. (1991) 'Cuttington University College during the Liberian civil war: An administrator's experience.' Liberian Studies Journal, XVI, p. 87.

Tuttle, K. (2003) The republic of Liberia. Retrieved in 2003 and available at: http://www.africana .com

Turner, J. H. (1991) The structure of sociological theory, fifth edition. Belmont, Ca: Wadsworth.

United Nations, Security Council (2004) Report of the panel of experts pursuant to paragraph 22 of Security Council Resolution 1521(2003) concerning Liberia.

Van Lange, P. A. H. (1997) Development of prosocial, individualistic, and competitive orientations: Theory and preliminary evidence, 73, 4, 733-746.

Victoria, M. and Associates (2000) From the learning organization to learning communities: Toward a learning society. Information series No. 382. ERIC DIGEST NO: 440294.

Von Glasersfield, E. (1995) A constructivist approach to teaching. In Steffe, L. and Gale, J. (Eds) Constructivism in education. New Jersey: Lawrence Elbaum Associates.

Vygotsky, L. (9178) Mind in society: The development of higher psychological processes. Cambridge: Harvard University Press.

Weick, K. E. (1982) "Administering education in loosely coupled schools". Phi Beta Kappan, 63, 10, 673-676.

Weiner, B. (1986) An attributional theory of motivation and emotion, Springer-Velag, New York.

Welton, M. (1995) In defense of the lifeworld: A Habermasian approach to adult learning. In Welton, M (Ed) In defense of the lifeworld: Critical perspectives on adult learning. New York: State University of New York Press.

Wilson, A. and Hayes, E. (2000) Handbook of adult and continuing education. San Francisco: Jossey-Bass.

Witkin, H. and Associates (1962) Psychological differentiation. New York: John Wiley and Sons.

Witkin, H. and Berry, J. (1975) Psychological differentiation in cross cultural perspective. Journal of Cross Cultural Psychology, 6, 5-87.

Witkin, H. and Goodenough, D. (9175) Field-dependent revisited. Princeton, NJ: Educational Testing Service.

Wlokowski, R. (1997) Motivation with a mission: Understanding motivation and culture in workshops design. In Flamming, J. (Ed) New perspectives on designing and implementing effective workshops. San Francisco: Jossey-Bass.

Wlokowski, R. (1997) Enhancing adult motivation to learn: A comprehensive guide for teaching all adults. San Francisco: Jossey-Bass.

World Bank (1982) "Staff appraisal report: Republic of Liberia fourth education project". Washington, D.C.

World Bank (2000) Attacking poverty. Oxford: Oxford University Press.

Wreh, T. (1976) The love of liberty: The rule of President William V.S. Tubman in Liberia 1944-1971. London: C. Hurst.

Wright, M. (1997) Japanese Universities and lifelong education: Trends and transitions. Paper presented at the annual conference of the comparative and international education society. University of Southern California, November, 14-15, 1997.

Yorks, L. and Marsick, V. (2000) Organizational learning and transformation. In Mezirow and Associates, Learning as transformation: Critical perspectives on a theory in progress. San Francisco: Jossey-Bass.

Index

About The Author

The author was born in Liberia, West Africa. During the past 18 years he had become truly a global citizen. He has studied and traveled to an array of Countries on four Continents including the United States. He completed his undergraduate and graduate studies in England and the United States. He has written widely on topical issues in the fields of education, policy and conflict studies. His articles have appeared over the years in Community-based news outlets, conference reports, as well as peer reviewed professional journals.